Entrepreneur®
MAGAZINE'S

start*up*

Start Your Own

STAFFING

SERVICE

Your Step-by-Step
Guide to Success

Entrepreneur Press, Krista Thoren Turner,
Alan Breznick, and Rachel Adelson

Ep
Entrepreneur.
Press

D0756947

Editorial Director: Jere L. Calmes
Managing Editor: Marla Markman
Cover Design: Beth Hansen-Winter
Production: Eliot House Productions
Composition: Ed Stevens

This publication is designed to provide accurate and authoritative information in regard to the subject matter covered. It is sold with the understanding that the publisher is not engaged ▇▇▇▇▇▇▇▇▇▇▇▇▇▇▇▇▇▇▇▇▇▇▇▇▇▇▇ vice or other ▇▇▇▇▇▇▇▇▇▇▇▇▇▇▇▇▇▇▇▇▇▇▇▇▇ erson ▇▇▇▇▇▇▇▇▇▇▇▇▇▇▇▇▇▇▇▇▇▇▇▇▇▇▇▇▇▇▇▇▇▇▇▇▇

Turn
  Start your own staffing service/Krista Turner.
     p. cm. —(Entrepreneur magazine's start up)
  Includes index.
  ISBN 1-891984-83-7
     1. Employee leasing service. I. Title. II. Series.

HF5549.5.E425T87 2003
331.12'8'0681—dc21   2003043952

10 09 08 07 06 05   10 9 8 7 6 5 4 3 2 1

Contents

Preface

Smith, Jones, and Johnson, Attorneys at Law, has an emergency. The firm's tax law division needs two additional corporate tax lawyers by tomorrow morning. At 3 P.M., the senior partner picks up the phone and calls you. Why? Because your firm, LawTemps Inc., can deliver two professional, competent lawyers who will fill the unexpected vacancies on a temporary basis. Smith, Jones, and Johnson will not need to advertise the positions, interview candidates, add employees to its payroll, or pay benefits. Your temporary staffing service has already handled those tasks.

After the call, you:

a. wake up sweating and are unable to go back to sleep.

b. play your "just imagine" game a little longer, sure that soon this will be you.

c. jump up and down, thrilled at getting your first client.

d. immediately spring into action and consult your availability list.

If you answered *a*, relax. Chances are you will never own a staffing service anyway because owners of these operations are fearless. So roll over, and go back to sleep.

If you chose *b*, however, this book is for you. With our help, you can make your dream of owning a staffing service a reality. And if you answered *c* or *d*, this book is also for you because even though you've already opened your doors for business, everyone needs new ideas.

Chapters 1 and 2 tell you what you need to know about the industry. Is it for you? What are the major rewards and challenges? What is a typical day like in the staffing industry? Chapters 3 through 7 cover the nuts and bolts of the business. You will learn about licenses, equipment, and financing options. You will also learn how to recruit and retain good employees. Finally, Chapters 8 through 10 show you how to make your staffing service a success. We will show you how to build a client base, promote your business and manage your finances. You will also learn how to avoid the common hazards of the industry.

This book includes some sample documents, worksheets, and other items to help you get started.

We have one very simple goal in writing this book—to give you, the reader, the information you need to start a staffing service. If you already own one, we'll help you make it even better. (Be sure to check out the troubleshooting tips and recommendations for success in Chapter 10.)

So have a seat, and let's get down to business. Your business.

1

Working It Out
Industry
Overview

This chapter focuses on the staffing industry and its niche markets. We'll tell you how some owners of staffing services got into the business, and we'll help you figure out if this kind of work is a good choice for you. Finally, we'll discuss the rewards and challenges of the industry and provide suggestions for conducting your own market research.

Sizing It Up

In this section, you'll learn what staffing services are all about and why the industry, which saw explosive growth during the 1990s but suffered during the recent economic slowdown, now seems poised for growth.

What They Are

Broadly speaking, staffing services are all of the following:

- *Employers.* Staffing services take on qualified candidates as employees. Such services not only pay their employees, but also withhold income tax and pay workers' compensation, disability, and unemployment insurance. Increasingly, staffing services also provide benefits such as vacation, personal time, health care, and retirement plans.

- *Businesses.* All companies have clients and products. In the staffing industry, clients are the companies that contract for labor or expertise, and the product is that very labor or expertise. The more skills that workers possess, the better the products these staffing services are able to provide for their clients. As with any company, staffing services are in business to make money, which they do either by adding their markup to all labor charges or by charging clients a finder's fee. Some services use a combination of these strategies.

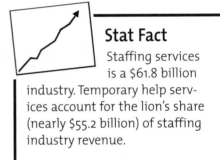

Stat Fact
Staffing services is a $61.8 billion industry. Temporary help services account for the lion's share (nearly $55.2 billion) of staffing industry revenue.

- *Contractors.* Temporary help and staffing services provide business organizations with employees for positions in all sectors of employment, from industrial to clerical to professional. In other words, staffing services match employees to client companies.

What They're Not

Staffing services are neither employment agencies nor professional employer organizations (PEOs). Although distinctions are blurring among the three types of companies, in most cases you will still find the following differences:

- *Employer status.* Staffing services are employers, while employment agencies and PEOs are not. When a staffing service sends an applicant to a company, the applicant becomes an employee of the staffing service, which assigns its employee to the client company for a specified length of time. On the other hand, once an employment agency matches an applicant with a company, the applicant becomes an employee of the company. PEOs typically take over the human resources functions of a company (e.g., payroll, insurance, etc.), leasing employees back to that company.

- *Service offerings.* Increasingly, lines are blurring among the three different types of companies in terms of the services they provide. However, staffing services offer training more consistently than the other two. Employment agencies still handle the majority of permanent placements. Finally, most PEOs are still, first and foremost, human resources specialists.

- *Recruiter status.* Both staffing companies and employment agencies recruit workers. Traditionally, PEOs have not handled recruiting but have instead taken charge of existing company employees, leasing them back to the company. Increasingly, however, PEOs have begun to offer recruiting services in addition to payroll, screening, and other more traditional services.

- *Fee assessment.* Staffing companies usually charge clients an hourly rate that includes labor plus a markup. Those that do temp-to-perm placement or

R.E.S.P.E.C.T.

The growth of the professional staffing sector has taken the temporary help industry to a whole new level of respectability. Gone is the stereotype of the temp who, unable to find a "real" job, settles for less. Temporary professional workers tend to be highly skilled and experienced individuals, often in their 40s or 50s. Many earn more than their former yearly salaries. Higher-end professionals may make $75,000 and up.

Recent corporate downsizing, the economic slowdown, and other bottom line-oriented business trends account in part for the growth in professional staffing. Nevertheless, many professionals are choosing temporary work as a means of gaining more control over their work lives. These individuals like the challenge, variety, and flexibility of temporary work. Some want a career change. Others want the flexibility they need for raising children. Still others want to reduce their work hours without retiring.

Even with the recent recession, the "free agent" work force has surged 27 percent since 1998, according to surveys conducted for Kelly Services, a leading global staffing company that serves 95 percent of *Fortune* 500 companies, and cited by the American Staffing Association. In 2002, free-agent workers accounted for 28 percent of the full-time U.S. work force, up from 22 percent in 1998 and 26 percent in 2000. There are now at least 30 million such workers in the nation.

permanent placement charge fees for that service. Employment agencies charge companies one-time fees for finding applicants. Of the three entities, employment agencies are the only ones that collect fees from applicants (although not all agencies do so).

- *Legal status.* Many states have no licensing requirements for staffing services. On the other hand, because employment agencies often collect fees from the applicants they place, these agencies are required to be licensed. Depending on the state, PEOs generally fall somewhere in between.

Stat Fact

Some 25 staffing companies cracked *Inc.* magazine's 2002 list of the 500 fastest-growing private companies in the United States. Of the 25 firms, four were in the top 100 and three were in the top 10. Integrity Staffing Solutions ranked highest among the firms, capturing second place overall.

Types of Staffing Services

Now that you know, in the very broadest sense, what a staffing service is (and isn't), let's discuss the different types.

- *Temporary staffing service.* This type of service makes up the largest chunk of the staffing industry and is the type of service discussed most in this book. Temporary staffing services supply client companies with workers on a short-term basis, either to fill in for absent employees or to supplement existing staff during particularly busy times.

- *Long-term staffing service.* This type of service, also known as "facilities staffing," specializes in placing employees in long-term assignments for indefinite periods of time. Project-related assignments, such as those found in the professional and technical sectors, often require long-term staffing.

- *Temp-to-perm staffing service.* This is a type of service seen more and more often, and one that is frequently combined with a temporary staffing service. A temp-to-perm staffing service offers clients a chance to try out a worker on a temporary basis and then hire that worker later if the client wishes to do so. In most cases, clients who hire a staffing service's employees pay a hiring fee for the privilege.

Although it is important to understand the distinctions among these types of staffing services, keep in mind that the lines dividing them have become indistinct and, in fact, have nearly disappeared. Many services do all types of staffing.

The industry gets even more interesting when you examine the different sectors within it. Some, like the office and clerical sector and the industrial sector, have

Medical Problems

Having a health-care background might make starting a medical staffing service seem like a logical choice. However, that niche might not be affordable for the following reasons:

○ *High administration costs.* Administrators in health care are very expensive because they have degrees.

○ *High training costs.* The personnel and medical equipment needed to supply temporary employees with ongoing training is expensive.

When you add up these factors, you have a very high start-up cost for a medical staffing service. But this is not the only barrier to entry. It can be hard to collect money from doctors and various agencies. For example, a nursing home might not pay for 120 days—and that's if it doesn't get sold or go out of business before paying you. Waiting for public funds to come through is a common scenario in the medical staffing industry. If you want to pursue this staffing sector, you'll need some serious financial resources, as well as patience.

been around since the beginning (see "The Temp Timeline" on page 9). Others, like the professional sector, are newer and still growing at phenomenal rates. We will touch on the various sectors again later in the chapter when we discuss finding your niche, but for now we'll provide a quick rundown. The staffing services industry is divided into the following three broad sectors:

- *Office/clerical.* Historically, this sector accounted for nearly half of all positions filled by temporary workers. But that has changed since the late 1990s in response to marketplace shifts and the recent recession. As a result, office/clerical now accounts for roughly one-third of the staffing industry's revenue and payroll. The sector covers the following positions: secretaries, general office clerks, receptionists, administrative assistants, word processing and data-entry operators, cashiers, etc.

- *Industrial.* This sector used to comprise the second-biggest chunk of positions filled by temp workers. But it is also on the decline as the U.S. economy shifts away from manufacturing. Like the office/clerical sector, the industrial area now generates about one-third of the staffing industry's revenue and payroll. It includes the following jobs: manual laborers, food handlers, cleaners, assemblers, drivers, tradesmen, machine operators, maintenance workers, etc.

- *Professional/technical.* This combined sector used to be broken into several smaller divisions, including professional, technical, health care, and marketing.

All these areas have been growing, thanks to shifts in the market as more people with higher skill and education levels look for the flexibility provided by temporary and contract work, and as the demand for these people increases. As in the first two sectors, the professional/technical area now accounts for about one-third of industry revenue and payroll. It covers a wide range of positions, including engineers, scientists, lab technicians, architects, technical writers and illustrators, draftsmen,

Stat Fact
The American Staffing Association estimates that publicly owned companies generate about half of the staffing services industry's revenue. But there are just 30 to 50 public firms nationwide; the vast majority are smaller, privately owned companies.

physicians, dentists, nurses, hygienists, medical technicians, therapists, home health aides, custodial care workers, accountants, bookkeepers, attorneys, paralegals, middle and senior managers, and advertising and marketing executives.

Growing Fast

This is a good time to be in the staffing industry. Despite the 2000-2002 economic downturn, the industry is picking up steam again, and future prospects are bright. In the first quarter of 2003, U.S. sales of temporary and contract staffing services rose 5 percent, to $13.1 billion, according to the American Staffing Association (ASA). That marked the third consecutive quarter of growth after six straight declining quarters.

The personnel supply services sector, which includes the staffing industry, is projected to grow rapidly over the rest of the decade as the economy expands. In fact, the U.S. Bureau of Labor Statistics (BLS) predicts that more jobs will be created in personnel supply services than in any other industry over the next few years. Further, BLS forecasts that personnel supply services will be the fifth fastest-growing industry through 2010.

There are approximately 7,000 to 9,000 staffing service firms in the nation, many of them very small. The list of firms changes each year as 1,000 or more go out of business or merge with others, while an equal number enter the business. "The barriers to entry are very low," says Steven Berchem, vice president of the ASA. "It costs almost nothing to open a staffing service. It's getting an office, a phone, and a computer system."

The 1,300-member ASA represents the staffing industry. About 1,000 of its members are actual staffing firms, while the others provide services to those firms. Members operate more than 15,000 offices and generate 85 percent of the industry's revenue. The organization has 69 chapters in 43 states and Washington, DC.

The following factors account for the staffing industry's strong growth during good economic times and its ability to withstand even the toughest recessions:

- *Labor shortage.* This may seem odd, but even in rough economic times, many companies have trouble finding workers with the proper skill sets. Firms also know that when the economy kicks into high gear again, they will face more pressing labor shortages, just as they did in the late 1990s. In addition, employers are concerned about upcoming labor shortages as baby boomers start to retire, leaving a smaller group of younger replacement workers.

- *Skills shortage.* The recent and continuing shift toward more service- and knowledge-based jobs has produced a shortage of skills in the U.S. labor market. Furthermore, rapid changes in technology mean that what is state-of-the-art today can be obsolete tomorrow and often so are the skills associated with that technology. Compounding the problem, companies cannot produce and stockpile service and knowledge as they used to be able to stockpile manufactured goods. Instead, companies rely on staffing services to help them cope with fluctuating demand.

- *Company policy changes.* Increasingly, companies want to achieve the following goals:

  - *Stay "lean and mean."* Hiring temporary workers allows companies to save themselves the hidden costs of employment (e.g., taxes, insurance, and benefits) that can add up to 25 to 40 percent of a worker's salary. As an added advantage, these companies incur no costs for absenteeism (because they pay only for the hours that the employee works).

  - *Streamline operations.* Companies increasingly look to staffing services to recruit and train full-time workers for them or to provide managed services for them (e.g., payroll, human resources, etc.). Outsourcing has become more and more common.

  - *Keep up employee morale.* Staff members view the policy of hiring temporary workers during busy times much more positively than they do a policy of hiring permanent workers and then firing them during hard times.

What's the Big Appeal?

It's easy to see why client companies like hiring temporary workers. But what's in it for the employees? At first glance, having a temporary job doesn't seem like much of a bargain. Yet for many people, joining a temporary staffing service offers the following advantages:

- *Flexibility.* Many people want control over when they work, where they work, and what kind of work they do. More people want the flexibility that comes with interim assignments. Individuals are increasingly going through more jobs over the course of a lifetime.

- *Opportunity.* A temporary assignment with a desirable company can be a good way to get a foot in the door. "Temporary jobs offer a bridge to permanent employment," says Richard Wahlquist, president and CEO of the ASA. "And more and more people are choosing employment with staffing firms as a career option."

- *Training.* Most staffing services provide training for their temporary employees. People who want to sharpen their skills or learn new ones often find this training an attractive perk.

Getting Into It

In this section, we'll provide suggestions on finding your niche and tell you how some staffing service owners got into the business.

Finding Your Niche

Traditionally, staffing services have operated in all sectors of employment. Older companies, such as Patty DeDominic's Los Angeles-based PDQ Personnel Services, tend to continue that tradition. Increasingly, however, staffing services operate within a niche market. The many specializations that exist today make the staffing industry much more complex, as well as far more interesting, than it has ever been before.

As you think about niche possibilities, consider the following factors:

- *Local supply and demand.* Staffing services need both temporary employees and clients to survive. Before you choose your niche, make sure you know the types of jobs available in your area and the potential labor supply. For example, if there are 10 factories in your town, don't rule out industrial placements. And every owner we talked to does some business in the office and clerical sector. Because this sector accounts for more than 30 percent of the industry, chances are good that virtually every staffing service will place office personnel, even if the major placement emphasis is elsewhere. Be aware, too, that there may be niches within a sector. For example, if you decide to focus on office and clerical positions, you'll find it's possible to specialize even further. Some staffing firms focus on providing midlevel administrative support staff to *Fortune* 500 companies. Others provide clients with higher-end office and clerical help.

Rita Zoller found that specializing in light industrial work was a natural choice for her Indianapolis-based First Call Temporary Service. "This is a heavy distribution center area," she says. She does some placements in the clerical, professional, and technical sectors, but most of her business is industry-related.

In Seattle, Dyana Veigele's Law Dawgs places a lot of high-demand legal secretaries, paralegals, and

Bright Idea

As your staffing service grows, consider offering other potentially lucrative services. For example, Seattle's Dyana Veigele, who owns Law Dawgs, has considered starting a training program for legal secretaries.

The Temp Timeline

○ *1890s.* This decade marks the first documented appearance of temporary workers in the United States on the shipping docks of Milwaukee, Wisconsin. Industrial temping begins.

○ *1920s.* Temporary staff appear in Chicago offices. Another sector of the industry gets its start.

○ *World War II.* Women leave their clerical jobs to take more lucrative factory jobs left vacant by men joining the armed forces. Temporary help firms recruit housewives to fill vacant clerical positions. This era marks the first appearance of services devoted to placing temporary employees.

○ *Post-WWII.* Temporary workers are discovered to be very valuable for replacing absent employees and for pitching in during periods of high labor demand.

○ *1970s.* The war in Vietnam, as well as a guns-for-butter economy, creates a huge demand for skilled manufacturing labor. Most temporary services still place primarily office and clerical or industrial workers.

○ *1990s.* The United States economy is the strongest it has been in three decades, and the demand for labor is the greatest since the Vietnam era. A shortage of skilled labor for service- and knowledge-based industries puts unprecedented demands on the staffing services industry.

○ *New millennium.* As the U.S. economy falters, demand plunges for temporary workers, staffing employment falls for 18 months, and sales drop 50 percent from their 2000 peak before the industry starts to recover.

lawyers. Her business does legal office support, from messengers and reception-ists to law partners and associates. It also covers everything in between, including secretaries, paralegals, word processors, and clerks.

- *Experience.* If you have a background in a particular field, this can be an advan-tage in several different ways. Not only will you be able to better assess appli-cants for jobs in that field, but your experience can also lend credibility to your staffing service. And you may feel more comfortable serving an industry with which you are familiar. For example, because Veigele is a lawyer, the legal staffing sector was a natural niche for her to pursue. Of course, familiarity and a high comfort level won't help if you can't find enough clients and employees, so you still need to do your market research.

- *Economic feasibility.* Sometimes a market niche that might be a natural choice given an entrepreneur's background isn't possible for financial reasons. For example, in spite of her medical background, one former owner chose not to open a medical staffing service due to its steep start-up costs. It can also be dif-ficult to get doctors, hospitals, nursing homes, and other medical institutions to pay in a timely manner. So that owner went into higher-end clerical instead.

Loving It

Staffing service owners seem to love what they do. They enjoy tackling new chal-lenges and tasks every day. Besides liking the variety, owners enjoy the people-ori-ented nature of the industry. Most of the owners we interviewed had industry experience before they started their own staffing service. We'll now take a quick look at their backgrounds.

In Chicago, Tallulah Noel started her career as a nurse, worked for a temporary staffing franchise called Nursefinders, and then helped build a home-care organiza-tion from the ground up before being laid off after a lengthy recuperation from a car accident. "I saw there was no safety net anywhere, so I realized I'd better take care of myself," she says. She launched Staffing Team International in 1994, placing mostly clerical personnel. The firm doubled in size each of its first few years and has long been debt-free. George Sotos bought Noel's business in 2002 and merged it with two other staffing firms.

Stat Fact
In the 1980s, roughly 165,000 temporary workers were employed each day. That num-ber has grown to approxi-mately 2.2 million.

Patricia Troy-Brooks put in 15 years at the executive level of two national staffing serv-ices before starting a service in 1995. Legal problems forced her to close her service mere days after opening it, but she was undaunted and started Advanced Staffing in downtown

Philadelphia in February 1996. "We had two desks and a telephone," she says. Almost immediately, her service won a multimillion-dollar contract with a Philadelphia-based insurance company. She moved her company to New Castle, Delaware, in the late 1990s as business grew.

Stat Fact

What are the biggest staffing services companies? Thanks to mergers and acquisitions, three firms now dominate the industry. They are Adecko, Manpower Inc., and Kelly Services, all publicly held.

Dyana Veigele started her legal staffing service in San Diego while she was still in law school. "I had a tax class and I came up with the idea and brought a friend in on it," she says. "It was a little thing we thought we would do during law school to place ourselves." Initially, they used only themselves and other law students as temporary workers. Before long, however, they were placing attorneys and legal secretaries as well, and their "little thing" had mushroomed into something big. "I actually took a leave of absence from law school to run the company," Veigele says, laughing. "We never placed ourselves. We placed everybody else." After she finished law school, she moved to Seattle, married, and opened her business there. She and her MBA husband are co-owners of Law Dawgs. Now in its eighth year, their company continues to grow.

Rita Zoller had substantial experience in staffing services before she started her Indianapolis business, First Call Temporary Services, with her daughter, who had just graduated from college. "My daughter and I decided to do this while we were shopping," she says. "I'd thought about it and I asked her if she wanted to go in with me." Zoller says having a family business has been fun. Their company is now in its 12th year, with five offices and 25 permanent staff members.

Patty DeDominic also had industry experience before starting PDQ Personnel Services in Los Angeles. Her company is now 24 years old and has California offices in Los Angeles and Irvine, as well as an East Coast office in Bridgewater, New Jersey. DeDominic has more than 30 permanent staff members.

Now you know how some owners got into the business. Rest assured, however, that a lack of industry experience does not mean you can't have a successful staffing service. It just means you'll need to do more research before you start your business. Your first step is to gather all the information you can about the industry. This is what the next section is all about.

Scoping It Out

In this section, we'll show you how to conduct market research, discuss the challenges you'll face, and examine changes that have recently taken place in the industry.

Market Research

A successful staffing company needs clients and workers. Therefore, the two major questions you must research are the following: (1) Does your area have enough companies of the type you'd like to have as clients? (2) Are there enough qualified workers in your area?

The "Conducting Market Research" chapter in *Start-Up Basics* provides a thorough discussion of ways to research the market. Many of the staffing service owners interviewed had backgrounds either in the staffing industry or in the industry their staffing company supports. These are both good ways to get a feel for local demand. Other good ways include:

Stat Fact

The American Society for Human Resources Management finds that more than 75 percent of companies surveyed say that meeting business demands is the primary reason they use alternative and temporary staff.

- *Interview potential client companies.* Find out how many temporary employees key companies use and how well their needs are currently being met. Ask if they would be interested in using an additional temporary help service. It is also important to find out patterns of usage because some businesses are seasonal in nature.

- *Check out existing services.* Consider signing on with one or more temporary services for a short time. This strategy will provide you with valuable insight into what it's like to be a temporary worker (assuming you don't already have experience). It will also give you a sense of how busy these services are, how satisfied their workers are, etc. (No, we are not suggesting that you spy. Merely test the water. Furthermore, be aware that you usually cannot work for another temporary service as a permanent employee without signing a noncompete agreement. For more on this topic, see the Glossary.)

- *Consult existing data.* Organizations like your local chamber of commerce and the Census Bureau offer information about the local population and businesses in your area.

Challenges

Every industry has special challenges. Although some of the problems we list below plague anyone who operates a business to some degree, they are particularly difficult problems for the staffing services industry.

Here are some of the major challenges you will face:

- *Cash flow.* The necessity of paying temporary employees before clients pay you is a particularly thorny problem in this industry. In Chapters 4 and 9, we provide suggestions for dealing with this problem.

- *Competition.* There has always been competition in the staffing services industry, but recently it has shifted in emphasis. Staffing firms now vie for both clients and applicants, making for a very competitive environment, particularly in a sluggish economy. In Chapters 5 through 8, you'll find ideas for setting your business apart from the rest of the competition.

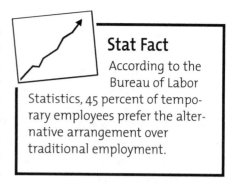

Stat Fact

According to the Bureau of Labor Statistics, 45 percent of temporary employees prefer the alternative arrangement over traditional employment.

- *Recruitment.* Surveys by the ASA show that recruitment is still a problem for today's staffing companies, even with relatively high unemployment rates. As we mentioned earlier in this chapter, there are three major reasons for the recruitment problem: (1) Despite higher unemployment, the cream of the crop is still tough to find, (2) client companies are pickier than ever about who they will take, and (3) today's workers need more skills than ever before.

    Staffing companies have had to work harder at recruiting. Many have also gotten more original. In Chapter 5, we give you ideas on how to beat the recruiting problem.

- *Retention.* Retaining employees once you've recruited them can also be a problem. Staffing companies have responded in several ways, including offering increased training opportunities. For more ideas on how to retain employees, check out Chapter 6.

Changing All the Time

Partly in response to the challenges we just discussed, the staffing services industry has seen several trends emerge over the last decade or so. These include:

- *Consolidation.* The ASA has witnessed a great deal of industry consolidation. New firms have been set up to do nothing but roll up groups of independents to make larger companies, to capitalize on economies of scale. Meanwhile, thousands of smaller firms have gone out of business since 2000, and franchisors have been buying out their franchisees.

- *Expansion of services.* More and more staffing companies have begun to offer additional services such as payroll, management services, permanent placement, and the training of clients' employees.

- *Roller-coaster growth.* The double-digit growth of the 1990s has been followed by large losses in the early part of this decade.

- *Specialization.* Staffing companies used to be generalists, serving all industry sectors. This is no longer true. Niche marketing is now the key, from the medical and legal sectors to the industrial and automotive industries.

"A lot of staffing firms are specializing," says one owner. "It wasn't that way ten years ago." She is amazed at the number of doctors and lawyers now placed as temporary employees. In addition, she finds that staffing companies have become much more professional and formal in the way they do business.

After reading this chapter, you should have a general idea of what the staffing services business is like. If we haven't sent you screaming in the opposite direction yet, read Chapter 2, which should do the trick.

Just kidding. Chapter 2 gets you closer to experiencing a day in the life of a staffing company. So read on.

Bright Idea

Consider joining the American Staffing Association (ASA), the recognized voice of the staffing industry. The ASA's 1,300 members operate 15,000 offices throughout the United States. The ASA offers industry statistics, seminars, journals, an annual convention, and other advantages to its members. For contact information, see the Appendix.

At Your Service
Day-to-Day Operations

In this chapter, we'll give you the information you need to run your business, as we take you behind the scenes for a look at how a staffing service operates on a daily basis. We'll also provide you with some samples of business forms typical of this industry.

▲

On the Front Lines

As a general rule, front-office work is "people work" and involves dealing with clients, employees, and applicants—in person, on the phone, or at the computer. Your sales staff will usually be out of the office by about 9 A.M. to drum up clients for you, so this section is about the "people work" those in the office (e.g., recruiters, employment counselors, coordinators, etc.) will be doing.

The Personal Touch

Most staffing services are open from 8 A.M. to 6 P.M., or some close approximation thereof. During this time, you should always have someone at the front desk, ready to greet those who walk in. The majority of people coming through your doors will be applicants, because clients rarely visit and most employees come in only occasionally (e.g., to pick up a paycheck).

When prospective employees come into your staffing service, you should do the following:

- *Ask what kind of job the candidate is looking for.* The response will tell you whether or not the prospective employee knows this information (many people—e.g., recent college graduates—don't know what they're looking for). The answer will also give you a hint as to whether the candidate has a resume.

- *Ask for a resume.* If you take a resume from a prospective employee, you should at least glance at it right away. Few things are more off-putting to a job seeker than handing out painstakingly assembled resumes, only to have them immediately tossed aside. Take a look at the education and job experience sections, at the very least. This resume will go into the file of the newly hired employee.

- *Ask for identification.* You need to see either proof of U.S. citizenship or a green card, because you cannot employ illegal aliens. Doing so has serious consequences. Get two forms of identification, at least one with a photo (e.g., a driver's license).

- *Collect paperwork.* All prospective employees should complete at least part of an application (the part that does not duplicate information already on a resume), a questionnaire, and a reference release form that allows their former employers to provide you with information. Standard applications are easily acquired through bookstores, office supply stores, or business schools. We supply a sample questionnaire and release form at the end of this chapter.

> ⚠ **Beware!**
> Avoid inconvenient, restrictive interviewing hours. In an era of stiff competition, the last thing you want to do is discourage potential employees.

- *Test likely candidates.* Depending on the job sought, prospective employees might be required to take a typing test, a spelling and grammar test, a math test, a computer knowledge test, and a special knowledge test (e.g., legal, medical, etc.). You can do all this testing on computers or some on paper. Standard proficiency tests are readily available in either software or paper form in bookstores or office supply stores. More specialized testing software is discussed later in this guide.

- *Interview successful applicants.* Someone who does well on all the tests is a good bet as a prospective employee. If possible, don't let such a person walk out the door without being interviewed. In these days of fierce competition for labor, your goal should be to get successful candidates signed up with your service the very day they walk in.

  So who does this interviewing on a moment's notice? Recruiters are the placement people, but it depends on who is available. Employment counselors also do some interviewing. When everybody else is busy, the owner interviews. Flexibility is key, aided by an open office layout.

- *Call employment references, and perform other necessary checks.* Front-desk personnel who aren't involved with the interview should be calling the applicant's references and performing other checks (background checks, educational checks, etc.). We discuss screening in detail in Chapter 5.

- *Provide some orientation.* Successful candidates who become new employees should be given orientation. Some staffing services, especially in the industrial sector, show films to all new employees. At the very least, you should hand employees a stack of time sheets, a business card, and an orientation packet. The latter doesn't need to be complicated, but you should have material that outlines what time they should call in their availability (usually first thing in the morning), explains how the time sheet system works, and informs them of any other special office procedures, including how and when

>
>
> **Beware!**
> Some staffing services do all their recruiting over the phone, which can lead to nightmarish stories. It takes face-to-face interviews to ensure that you're recruiting quality employees. "I've seen God on paper," says Dyana Veigele. "And then he walks into the office, and I wouldn't place him."

> **Smart Tip**
> Be aware that prospective employees will be looking for the following: a friendly office atmosphere, considerate treatment of current temporary employees, an interested interviewer who listens well, and orientation information that is clear and well-stated.

they'll be paid. You should provide a list of legal dos and don'ts (see "An Ounce of Prevention" on page 115 in Chapter 10). Your material should also list your responsibilities to your employees—as well as theirs to you. For some sample orientation material, check out the end of this chapter. Any pieces of information that are especially important for the smooth running of your office (e.g., availability calls, time sheet deadlines) should appear in more than one place in your material, preferably highlighted or in bold print. You may also want to tell new employees that this information is particularly important.

Calling All Personnel

Once your staffing service is up and running, you will no longer be sitting around waiting for the phone to ring. In fact, you (and your employees) can expect to spend a lot of time on the phone, especially in the morning, when staffing services invariably buzz with activity. So who, exactly, will be phoning you? Prospective employees, current employees, and clients—that's who. They'll be calling you to accomplish the following:

- *Request information.* New candidates call about signing on as temporary workers. Encourage them to come in and apply.

- *Report availability.* Temporary employees call to let you know they are available for assignment. All names should be put onto your availability list, also known as a "hot list." Most staffing industry software (see Chapter 7) allows for easy creation of this type of list.

- *Call in a time sheet.* Some temporary employees call in their time sheets, especially if they are running late on a payroll deadline. Take down the hours and give them to your payroll division, but let employees know you need a hard copy (faxed or mailed) with the client company signature before issuing a paycheck.

- *Place a work order.* Client companies call to request temporary employees. Assuming you are fairly sure you can produce an employee, tell them you will get back to them within a half-hour (or an hour, or whatever your call-back time range is). Then make sure you do phone them, even if it's to report that you'll need a bit more time to find someone.

Once you have an employee and an agreement with the client on a billing rate (see Chapter 9 for how to price your services), make sure you take down the following information: company address and phone number, job description, supervisor's full name and phone number, dress code, start date, daily start and finish time, length

Bright Idea

Used judiciously, phone calls to existing clients informing them about new employees or new training methods that might interest them can be an effective way to touch base with clients. Make sure also to ask clients what skills they wish they could find in employees.

of the assignment, and department to which the employee should report. Clients will probably let you know what, if any, special requirements they have (e.g., a temporary employee with industry experience or security clearance), but you should ask anyway.

If you don't have the employee a client needs, you have a choice. You can call back and suggest that the client try another service. Or, preferably, you can call another service yourself and arrange to give them the work order on the condition that they don't deal directly with the client. This solution (see Chapter 8 for information on networks with other services) minimizes the risk that you'll lose the client to the other service.

(see Chapter 8 for information on networks with other services)

- *Cancel a work order.* When a client cancels an assignment, some staffing services charge a four-hour minimum fee. The employee may get two-hour time-and-trouble pay.

- *Report a crisis.* Both clients and temporary employees call to report problems. Client problems include no-show workers, billing questions, or dissatisfaction with workers. Temporary employee problems include dissatisfaction with a job and inability to report to an assignment (e.g., employee is sick or has another emergency).

These categories should cover most of the calls your office receives on a typical morning. But incoming calls are only half of the picture. Outgoing calls are the other half. Your office will make a lot of these. And once again, mornings are the time. Following are some of the types of calls you and your front-desk personnel can expect to make:

- *Arrival calls.* Most owners call clients to make sure that temporary employees have arrived. The majority of these calls are made in the morning. "We make arrival calls for every position we fill," says Patty DeDominic of LA's PDQ Personnel Services. In Seattle, Law Dawgs' owner Dyana Veigele makes occasional arrival calls. "It just depends on who we're placing and the sensitivity we have with that client, too," she says. "Some clients we've worked with forever, and they'll let us know [if an employee doesn't arrive].

Beware!
You should be aware that rival staffing companies may call, posing as potential clients, to find out details about your business (e.g., billing rates). This practice is called "shopping."

Smart Tip
Every industry sector has idiosyncrasies. Find out what the standard operating procedures are for the niche in which you'll be working. For example, many legal and professional staffing services require resumes to be sent through the mail (either electronic or United States Postal Service variety). Once an assignment match is found, candidates interview with the service. The staffing service then submits a short list to the client company, which interviews the candidates.

▲

Believe me. With others, you have to give them the comfy cozy stuff."

- *Second-day calls.* A few staffing services also make second-day calls to clients to make sure everything is still going smoothly. However, most clients prefer not to be bothered with additional calls. "People are too busy," observes Rita Zoller in Indianapolis, who owns First Call Temporary Services.

- *Placement calls.* Once you have made a match, call the employee and offer the position. Make sure to give them the following info: job description, company name and address, pay rate, start date and time, hours per day, and length of assignment. If the employee accepts the assignment, then provide the supervisor's name, title, and phone and extension number. Also let the employee know about the dress code and the job's location within the building (i.e., floor and suite number). Finally, make sure you give the employee a work order number to put at the top of the time sheet. The work order number is supplied by your service and used for tracking purposes.

> ## Smart Tip
> *Tip...*
>
> On a very busy morning, you and your staff may have trouble covering all the incoming calls. If this is the case, don't try to log employees' availability into the computer. Just have the receptionist or someone from the back office write down the names of those available.

Accept that employees will turn down assignments, even in the current climate of economic uncertainty. An assignment may be turned down for any of the following reasons and more: The applicant has a schedule conflict, thinks the pay is too low, or simply doesn't want that kind of job.

If the employee declines the assignment, don't despair. Just call another person. And because a refusal is not a rare occurrence, you should always jot down the name of more than one employee you can call, especially if the computer gives it to you.

- *Replacement calls.* If an employee calls in sick or, for whatever reason, is unable to take an assigned position, you and your office staff members must first inform the client and then find a replacement for that employee. Make sure you do this as fast as possible. Quick replacement should be a top priority.

- *Courtesy calls.* Most staffing services call clients weekly (usually on Fridays) to touch base with them. "It's important to stay in touch," says Patty DeDominic, who terms them "quality control follow-up calls." A similar recommended practice is to call clients soon after sending

> ## Smart Tip
> *Tip...*
>
> In an industry that relies heavily on phones for conducting business, it is crucial to make sure all your staff members practice good telephone etiquette. You want callers to have a good impression of your company.

out invoices, to build rapport and boost customer service. An administrative coordinator can call to make sure there are no problems with the bill and to see if the client needs anything.

- *Sales calls.* In addition to calling prospective clients, some staffing services call existing clients. You can generate new business by calling current clients to let them know about available workers and their skills.

- *Follow-up calls.* Not all services make these calls, but most owners recommend calling all temporary employees several days into their assignments. Follow up to determine if the job was as quoted; if for some reason it's not, you can then call the customer. Also consider calling the employee sometime within the first week to find out how the job is going and whether the employee has learned any new skills. Then update the employee's file.

Smart Tip

Tip...

Many staffing services offer guarantees on their employees. If a client calls within a specified time limit (usually four hours) and indicates dissatisfaction with an employee, the staffing service either refunds the four-hour fee or replaces the employee. It is always a good idea to call and make sure clients are satisfied with the employees you've supplied, but it is especially important to call if your service offers this guarantee.

- *Verification calls.* While the prospect is taking the computerized tests, your staff can call the references. After that, employees get set up to work while your agency calls an investigator such as Pinkerton's to start the background check. Employment depends upon a clean record. Pinkerton's is a nationwide investigations and security company based in Encino, California.

The Matching Game

The task of matching employees to client requests is also "people work," if in a more abstract form. And if you start with a small business, you may get to know quite a few of your temporary employees fairly well.

Once you know what skills and other qualities the client wants, the next step is to match that information to the employee who provides the best fit. This match may be achieved by computer or by hand, depending on the size of your service. Selection criteria include the following—beginning with those that are, relatively speaking, the most important:

- *Availability.* Check the availability list. (You do have one, don't you? Take advantage of the fact that most industry-specific software allows you to easily create "hot lists.")

- *Skills.* Computerized matching makes it a lot easier to compare the requested skills with the skills of available employees. For a discussion of software available to help you with your matching tasks, see Chapter 7.

- *Career goals.* A good staffing service cares about the career goals of its employees, both permanent and temporary. You should take every chance you get to give a deserving and capable employee experience in a desired field of work.

- *Pay rate.* Make sure you look at employees' stated acceptable pay ranges. There is no point in wasting time calling an employee with a job offer that pays less than what that employee is willing to accept. If the client is especially valuable, however, and you are desperate to fill the position, consider negotiating with the employee.

> **Tip...**
>
> **Smart Tip**
>
> Time clocks are another way to establish that your employees are where they're supposed to be, when they're supposed to be there. Rita Zoller's company takes them on-site. This strategy is common when large numbers of temporary employees are working at the same company, as is often the case in the industrial sector.

- *Length of the assignment.* This criterion is important not only because of the availability issue (i.e., potential scheduling conflicts) but also because some employees are more suited to short-term assignments, while others work out better in long-term assignments. For example, recent college graduates who don't know what they want to do are probably best served by short-term positions, as are those who are either changing careers or back in the work force after a long absence. On the other hand, longer assignments will probably better suit those who are between jobs.

- *Attitude/personality.* Employee answers to your questionnaire (see the end of this chapter) and to interview questions may help you make the right match. For example, employees who prefer a laid-back atmosphere are probably not a good match for a company trying to meet an urgent deadline.

- *Location.* For some employees, transportation may be a problem. Others may prefer not to work in certain locations. Both of these considerations apply more often in large cities.

- *Seniority level.* Employees who have been with your service for six months or more should get first crack at more desirable positions.

What if you or the computer come up with more than one match? This is a good situation, actually. It means you have several chances to find a suitable worker. After all, the first person you call (and even the second or third) may decline the position. But how will you decide whom to call first?

Use the following strategies:

- *Check all employees' resumes or your computerized record of their work.* Someone may have more experience in the type of job you're trying to fill.

- *Check evaluations of all employees.* Who delivers the best on-the-job performance?
- *Offer the job first to the qualified employee with the greatest seniority.*

At the Bargaining Table

Negotiation is both an art and a skill. As such, it is the subject of many clever, insightful books. This is not one of them. What we do here is simply point out that negotiation is important "people work" and that you'll need to do some of it with clients and employees alike. Here are some points that will come under discussion:

- *Billing rate.* A company that does a high volume of business with you may expect a reduced billing rate. All owners we spoke to give lower billing rates to volume customers—and sometimes to customers who have been with them a long time.
- *Pay rate.* Your personnel coordinator, or whoever else phones employees with assignment offers, should have the authority to decide on the spot whether or

---

Diary of a Coordinator

8:00 A.M. Call from temp running late (car trouble). I jot down name, company.

8:00 A.M. XYZ company frantic. Must have three people immediately, preferably yesterday.

8:02 A.M. Employee lost. Needs directions to job site. I give directions, call company about tardiness (they're thrilled), look up availability list for XYZ work orders.

8:03 A.M. Arrival call to Alpha Co. Uh-oh. Temp not there—over an hour late. Assure them I'll flush him out or send a replacement.

8:04 A.M. Wherever he is, he's not at home. Got our faithful Susan to replace him—hooray! Now more calling on those XYZ work orders. Very high-tech, specialized stuff. This won't be a piece of cake....

8:25 A.M. Must phone XYZ now so we make our 30-minute call-back guarantee. Have gotten two out of three workers they need. Will keep trying.

8:25 A.M. Call from prospective applicant who is not sure if temp work is for her. On the one hand, she really likes people and would just love going to lots of different companies. She could be a receptionist, maybe, or a secretary. She asks if we hire for any vets because she loves animals and is really good with them. On the other hand, she's not too hot with computers because her mom won't let her get one. Bummer, huh? But maybe computers aren't too important?

I tell her that, actually, computers are very important and so is finishing high school. We need highly skilled workers, and she should make sure to give us a call once she graduates.

not to agree to an employee's request for a higher pay rate on an assignment. If the employee is a good one or the job is tough to fill and the client is valuable, paying a higher rate may be worth it.

- *Payment schedule for accounts receivable.* This is an important negotiating point. Unless you have a funding or factoring company (see Chapter 4) to help you with your cash flow (or unless you are independently wealthy), negotiate the shortest possible time frame within

Stat Fact

The percentage of accepted work orders for which staffing companies are able to provide employees is called the fill rate. Usually, it is impossible to fill every request. However, staffing services aim for an average fill rate of at least 85 percent.

which to receive the money that clients owe you. It may even, especially at the beginning, be worthwhile to accept a lower billing rate in return for prompt payment.

- *Transportation.* If an assignment poses a transportation difficulty for an employee (e.g., a night job can make public transportation risky or impossible), you may need to negotiate travel costs with your client.

Behind the Scenes

Back-office duties often involve an immense amount of paperwork, much of it computerized, rather than dealing with people. Industry-specific software can make back-office tasks less onerous and time-consuming.

Back-office work falls into the following categories:

- *Accounts payable.* All your company expenses, including employee paychecks, utility bills, and other expenses, are handled through accounts payable.

- *Accounts receivable.* This is money your clients owe you. You'll need to generate invoices, bill clients, and keep a close eye on aging receivables (i.e., overdue payments). The more they age, the less likely you'll get your money. Expect to make phone calls and write letters to remind clients they need to pay you.

- *Benefits.* This task involves keeping track of employee insurance, vacations, retirement plans, etc.

Smart Tip

Tip...

Keep your files tidy and the number of them manageable. For example, you might keep temporary employees active (i.e., in the computer) for a year. After that, your staff can purge the files. They're not gone forever, but they are out of the computer and the front-office space.

- *Payroll.* Remember that as the employer, you must figure out all federal, state, local, and employee tax deductions. Usually, time sheets are due in by the Monday following the week in which the employee worked. Most staffing services do payroll the first half of the week and distribute checks on Fridays.

Bright Idea

Consider getting another company to do your payroll. Law Dawgs has outsourced its payroll from the start. "It's easier that way," says owner Dyana Veigele. By having another company handle payroll, she saves herself from having to add staff.

The Tortoise or the Hare?

What, you may ask, are the busiest (and slowest) days in this industry? What about the months? Will the summer months find you racing for the finish line or plodding along at a calm pace? The short answer to these questions is: It depends. It depends on your market niche and the companies you serve.

Here goes the long answer:

Many services find that Monday, Tuesday, and Wednesday are heavy days for filling orders. Services that handle a lot of project work often get emergency work orders at the end of the week, because most projects are due on a Friday. For many services, Friday afternoons are busy, with orders coming in for the following week. Staffing services that distribute paychecks on Fridays often have a midweek rush to get payroll done.

As for those summer months, if your service provides personnel for what are termed "essential positions" (i.e., positions that must be kept covered), you can probably expect to be busy during the summer, when many permanent staff members take their vacations. On the other hand, if you provide high-end clerical support, you may well find that the summer months are slower for you, because executives also take their vacations then and thus do not need office assistance.

But what about the rest of the year? Remember that tourist seasons can have surprisingly far-reaching effects. And if you supply staff to the retail industry, expect that the holiday season will be busy for you, beginning well before Thanksgiving.

See what we mean? It really does depend, to a large extent, on your market niche. Allow yourself some time to figure out what the busiest days and months are for you. Then adjust your schedule so that you attack those tasks you can control (e.g., producing graphs) during calmer periods.

- *Reports.* To generate reports, you'll need to gather a lot of information and maybe even graph data (e.g., markup, number of job orders, fill ratio, etc.).
- *Supplies.* Simply put, whoever is in charge of this job needs to make sure your business doesn't run out of any office supplies.

Front- and back-office tasks are both crucial to the operation of a staffing service. Owners we talked to did both types of work during a typical day. Your time might be divided 50/50 between people work and paperwork.

Beware!
Make sure your payroll procedures result in accurate checks for your employees. Mistakes regarding hours worked, pay rate, and amount of overtime can give your service a bad reputation. If you outsource your payroll function, be prepared to look for another provider if you discover consistent errors.

Top Form

We've given you a look at the inner workings of a staffing service. Now we provide you with samples of some of the forms you'll need for your business. These forms include:

- Sample questionnaire
- Sample reference release form
- Sample orientation material—Q&A
- Sample orientation material—responsibilities
- Sample time sheet
- Sample invoice

We hope this chapter has given you a better idea of what goes on at a staffing service. It's now time to turn our attention to what you need to do to get your own business up and running. So grab a strong cup of coffee and read on as we tackle the necessary paperwork.

Sample Questionnaire

New Millennium Staffing Inc.

1. Have you done temporary work before?   Yes_____   No_____

   If you answered "Yes," please answer questions A-C.
   a. For which service(s) have you worked?

   _____
   _____

   b. Did you like temporary work?

   _____

   c. What type of work did you do?

   _____
   _____

2. Why are you interested in doing temporary work?

   _____
   _____

3. Approximately how many hours would you like to work per week?

   _____

4. What are your preferred days/times to work?

   _____

5. Are you willing to travel? How far?

   _____

6. What are your pay requirements?

   _____

7 What type of work environment do you prefer? Busy or laid-back?

   _____

8. What special skills can you offer when you go out on a job?

   _____
   _____
   _____

Sample Reference Release Form

New Millennium Staffing Inc.

To: _____

Re: _____

I authorize you to release true and honest reference information about me to New Millennium Staffing Inc.

_____
      Applicant's signature   Date

The above individual has applied to us for the position of _____
Your name has been given as an employer reference for the time period ___
_____
According to your records:
What were the dates of employment?_____
What was the employee's position?_____
_____
Would you rehire this individual?_____
_____
Comments: _____
_____
Your signature, title: _____
Company: _____
Dated: _____

We thank you very much for providing us with this information.

Sincerely,

New Millennium Staffing Inc.

Sample Orientation Material—Q&A

New Millennium Staffing Inc.
WE'RE GLAD YOU ASKED!

Here are some answers to frequently asked questions:

Q: How do I get an assignment?
A: When we get a client request for an employee matching your skills and interests, we'll call you.

Q: When will I be assigned work?
A: Just as soon as we can match you. Our goal is to keep you working at jobs you enjoy.

Q: Once I'm on the job, are you still my employer?
A: Yes, we are! We pay your wages and provide any benefits you're entitled to.

Q: When will I get paid?
A: The Friday after your workweek.

Q: What are the time sheets for?
A: They list the hours you worked that pay period. We use them to figure out your pay. That's why we need them by the Monday before payday.

Q: Can I ever get a raise?
A: Sure! We like to reward good work.

New Millennium Staffing Inc.

OUR RESPONSIBILITIES TO YOU

We will do the following:

○ Treat you courteously at all times

○ Keep you working as much as we possibly can

○ Provide training so that you can improve current skills and learn new ones

○ Work with you to help you meet your career goals

○ Deliver accurate paychecks to you on time

○ Accord you all benefits once you qualify for them

YOUR RESPONSIBILITIES TO US

You are responsible for doing the following:

○ *Completing assignments.* Barring illness, dire emergency, or a job that lasts longer than originally stated, you are expected to complete assignments you've agreed to undertake.

○ *Providing notice.* If the length of an assignment gets extended such that you cannot complete it, make sure you let us know as soon as possible.

○ *Posting in.* Call your personnel coordinator within the first few hours on the first day of an assignment.

○ *Verifying time sheets.* Make sure your time sheets contain the correct number of hours worked, are signed by the client company, and are handed in on time.

○ *Reporting availability status.* If you are about to finish an assignment, please let us know. Conversely, if the client company asks you to stay beyond the completion date of an assignment, give us a call. If you are sick or planning to go on vacation, please inform us of your nonavailability status.

○ *Following our rules.* Observe the rules listed on your time sheet regarding actions you may not take on the job. These include, but are not limited to, handling money and operating machinery without our written consent.

○ *Calling to report anything unusual.* If you are asked to stay past normal quitting time (i.e., work into a second shift) or to perform a function outside the range of your agreed-upon tasks, you should inform us of this. We may need to negotiate new terms with the client company (possibly with higher pay for you). If you are ever involved in a work-related accident or feel that something is wrong at the assignment location, make sure to call us.

Sample Time Sheet

New Millennium Staffing Inc.

oo Century Blvd. • Normal, IL 61761
Phone: (000) 345-5555 • Fax: (000) 234-5555

Name _____

Social Security # _____ Work order # _____

Week beginning (month, day, year) _____

Client company_____

Supervisor's signature, title _____

I certify that the hours listed above are correct and that I have sustained no injuries related to my duties on the job.

_____
Employee signature

	Monday	Tuesday	Wednesday	Thursday	Friday	Saturday	Sunday	Total Hours
Hours Worked								
Overtime Hours								
						Total Weekly Hours		

Please note that New Millennium Staffing employees may not do any of the following while at a client work site:

○ Handle cash or other valuables   ○ Operate alone on the premises

○ Operate machinery or motor vehicles
   without the written consent of the service

Fold along line, seal, stamp and send to the address below.

_____

_____

_____

Postage
Required

New Millennium Staffing Inc.
oo Century Blvd.
Normal, IL 61761

Sample Invoice

New Millennium Staffing Inc.
oo Century Blvd. • Normal, IL 61761
Phone: (000) 345-5555 • Fax: (000) 234-5555

INVOICE #3007

TO: John Doe & Sons
        Anytown, CA 55555

DATE: June 11, 200x

TEMPORARY SERVICE CHARGES FROM 6/1/0x TO 6/7/0x

Jim Smith, computer programmer, work order #221-5
  20 hours worked @ $50/hr. $1,000.00

               TOTAL AMOUNT DUE   *$1,000.00*

FULL AMOUNT DUE AND PAYABLE UPON RECEIPT

First Things First
Laying the Groundwork

If the previous chapter didn't turn your hair gray, then chances are you're good with details—in which case the staffing industry may be perfect for you. This chapter provides information about what you'll need to do before you look for financing (the topic of Chapter 4). First up is the creation of a business plan. Next, we'll discuss choosing a name and location for your business. Finally, we'll take a quick look at legal matters such as determining your business structure and acquiring the necessary licenses and insurance. (Don't think we can't see your eyes glazing over. Go get that cup of coffee. This stuff may not be riveting, but it's definitely important.)

Getting Creative

All of the tasks discussed in this section require you to think about what your staffing service will be like. That's not always easy, especially if you're still at the drawing board stage. So take a deep breath and set your imagination free. (No, we didn't say let it run wild. Just give it a little latitude.)

Get with the Plan

Why do you need a business plan? Quite simply, because a good one will help you do three things: manage your business, communicate your ideas, and gain financing. A business plan is crucial for any company and must frequently be revised in response to changing conditions. All the owners we spoke with had business plans.

Your own plan should include a discussion of the staffing services industry. This is where you'll use some of the most relevant data you gathered during your research. (See? There really is a use for that research. If necessary, go back to Chapter 1.) Your plan should also mention your business structure (stay tuned); the service you will offer; who your clients will be; the competition and how you expect to beat it; your income and cash flow (stay tuned for that, too); and other financial information.

All businesses should have a mission statement, and often this is included as part of the business plan. A good mission statement expresses your company's philosophy and helps keep you focused on the goals of your staffing service. Ask yourself the following questions:

- What kind of customer service will my company provide?
- What role will my staffing service play in the industry?
- What are my goals for my company's future?

Staffing service owners stress the importance of a mission statement. "Our philosophy is to give clients the best service they've ever had at a fair price and to enhance the life of anyone who walks through our doors," says Rita Zoller, who runs First Call Temporary Service in Indianapolis.

> **Bright Idea**
> Look in the Yellow Pages under "Employment—Contractors" and choose a name that puts your company at or near the top of the alphabetical list. This way, people who are letting their fingers do the walking may end up strolling through your doors (i.e., calling your company) first.

Patty DeDominic, who owns PDQ Personnel Services in Los Angeles, says her mission statement is more of a vision of what her company should be: "The standard for excellence in service, quality, and innovation."

A good business plan will be well worth the effort you put into it. The "Business Plan" chapter in *Start-Up Basics* provides in-depth instructions to help you create a winning plan.

A Rose by Any Other Name

A rose may smell sweet no matter what its name, but the same cannot be said of your business. The wrong moniker can get you either overlooked or bypassed, either of which fate can spell doom for your fledgling staffing service. When choosing a name, consider each of the following aspects of your company:

- *Scope.* Do you expect your business to expand to other locations? If so, you should rule out a name that includes your town or state. Tallulah Noel named her company Staffing Team International in hopes that the name would give her dream of eventually opening a foreign office a better chance of becoming a reality.

- *Niche identification.* Making your specialization clear ensures that potential clients and employees can easily find you. It also helps minimize time spent directing unsuitable clients elsewhere. Dyana Veigele and her husband included the word "law" in the name they chose for their legal staffing service, Law Dawgs.

- *Attributes.* You may want to stress an important feature of your staffing company. For example, Patty DeDominic chose PDQ Personnel Services because it implies speedy service. In an industry whose clients need workers quickly, this is a good choice.

- *Philosophy.* If teamwork is important, consider using the word "team" in your company name.

After you've drawn up a short list of ideas, look at each name and ask yourself the following questions:

- *Is it easy to pronounce?* People are sometimes reluctant to say a name they're unsure how to pronounce. Because you want your company name repeated, and often, do your best to ensure that it rolls easily off the tongue. Of course, if your family name is a tongue twister but you feel strongly about using it, go ahead. (Just don't blame us.)

Bright Idea

If your staffing service has a unique name, you may want to consider trademarking that name, as did Law Dawgs' Dyana Veigele and her husband. Get the facts about registering a trademark by consulting your local library or by calling the U.S. Government Printing Office at (888) 293-6498 and requesting the brochure *Basic Facts about Trademarks.* You can also order it online at http://bookstore. gpo.gov.

- *Is it short enough?* Besides the fact that length affects ease of pronunciation, keep in mind that clients who call you usually want personnel yesterday.

- *Is it easy to spell?* Avoid a name that's tough to look up in the phone book.

Rita Zoller says that in the end, it was her daughter who came up with their company name, First Call Temporary Service. "I think we were actually at the Red Lobster drinking wine," she says with a chuckle. Which brings us to the point that you should do whatever (legal) activity it takes to inspire you. If trying to come up with a suitable moniker has left you feeling worn and frazzled, do something relaxing. A glass of wine, a warm bath, or a chocolate bar can all have a soothing effect, allowing your brain cells to do their work. The result? You'll discover the brilliant name your business deserves.

> **Smart Tip** Tip...
>
> Check out the Yellow Pages listings of other staffing services. Make sure your name isn't too similar to that of an existing company. Also, look for ways to make your name stand out. For example, if most services use the word "staff" in their name, try using "personnel" instead.

Location, Location, Location!

This saying might hail from the real estate industry, but it is equally true for the staffing industry. Office location does matter and, generally speaking, your home is not a good one. Assuming your employee pool will not be limited to close friends and family, you need a professional atmosphere in which to test applicants, interview likely candidates, train employees, and hold the occasional business meeting.

Generally speaking, anything from a strip mall location to a street-front location to an office in an industrial park can work for a staffing service. Before you begin looking, you should have a clear picture of what you want and what you're able to pay. As you scope out possible territory, consider all of the following:

- *Image.* Seattle-based Dyana Veigele finds that location can be extremely important to image in the legal industry. That's why she and her husband located Law Dawgs in one of the main bank buildings in downtown Seattle. "We want to let the candidates who come in to interview know that we are professionals—that we are upscale legal placement," she says. So they chose their office building to fit that image. "It's expensive," admits Veigele, "but we really felt that was extremely important." She feels their decision has paid off.

- *Client proximity.* On the theory that where there are clients, there will also be workers, sometimes choosing your location based on the clientele you'd like to attract is a good plan. For instance, a staffing service in Chicago could support corporate giants such as Ace Hardware, McDonald's, Platinum Technologies, and Inland Realty. Similarly, Veigele says her company's sole office is in downtown Seattle partly because downtown is the hub of legal activity.

- *Accessibility.* It's important that your location be easy for potential employees to reach. Choose your location with recruiting in mind. Rita Zoller in Indianapolis, for example, chose her location for accessibility. "Our biggest concern is being in an area that's good for our employee population, because the clients come into our office very rarely. We go to theirs." She chose an office near a light industrial area, where such workers are likely to live.

> **Bright Idea**
>
> Consider starting your company in an executive office suite, which will provide you with a good business address, a professional atmosphere, and equipment such as phones, photocopiers, and fax machines. Executive office suites are extremely suitable for the staffing industry.

- *Economic feasibility.* You may need to minimize overhead. "One of our competitors has an office outside of the downtown area, under the highway, and he gets away with it," says Law Dawgs' Veigele. "His overhead is very low."

- *Expansion possibilities.* Keep in mind that your business will (you hope) grow. A location that provides room for expansion can be very important, because moving is expensive. For instance, Law Dawgs' bank-building location makes expansion possible. "We have offices available to take on, and more suite area. But we started out in one small office," Veigele says.

Patricia Troy-Brooks also started small (one room) and expanded later. Her company, Advanced Staffing, is still expanding. Several years ago, it took over some space from a neighboring business, expanding its own space to 3,300 square feet.

She was thankful that her firm didn't have to move. "You know what it would have cost us to have to move our location and change our stationery?" Big bucks, she says.

If you plan for growth, take steps right from the beginning to make sure you have room to expand. For example, you can negotiate a lease that gives you first rights to any adjacent units so you can take them without waiting for someone else to move out.

> **Bright Idea**
>
> Depending on your market niche, it may be wise to locate your business near an employment office, training center, higher-education facility, or retirement center. One of Rita Zoller's Indianapolis offices, for instance, used to be in the same building as the employment office and job training services. You can also maximize employee accessibility by locating your service near a bus line.

- *Lease flexibility.* If you are starting small, such that moving would not be an expensive disaster, it's a good idea to consider temporary space for the first few months of your company's life. If you discover you've made a mistake, you don't want to be locked into a long lease. Make sure the landlord will negotiate and work with you. Essentially, before you sign on the dotted line, everything in the lease is subject to negotiation.

Legal Ease

As with any new business, opening a staffing service will require you to jump through some legal hoops. We hope this section will make some of those hoops more navigable for you.

Structural Integrity

Small businesses usually take one of the following forms: sole proprietorship, general partnership, limited partnership, corporation, or limited liability company. The "Business Structure" in *Start-Up Basics* discusses all these forms in detail. Some staffing services are sole proprietorships, but most are corporations. We'll do a brief review of these two forms.

A sole proprietorship is probably not a good bet in this industry. Sole proprietors are personally responsible for any debt incurred by the company. Liability is a big problem for the staffing services industry. If a client or a worker sues your company, it is best not to have your personal assets attached. An additional consideration is the fact that most banks are not eager to lend money to sole proprietorships.

A corporation is probably the way to go. Incorporating your business protects your personal assets. The hitch is you might pay federal taxes twice, because the corporation gets taxed and then you get taxed again on your own income from your business. Filing a subchapter S election with the IRS can completely solve the double federal taxation problem (although, depending on the state, it may not work for state taxes).

Because of the federal tax relief the S corporation provides, most of the owners we spoke to chose this form. "For a small business, for tax purposes, it was really just the best decision," says Indianapolis-based Rita Zoller. "I would venture to say most start-ups [in the industry] are S corporations." She and her daughter had a CPA and an attorney help them decide on First Call Temporary Service's business structure.

If deciding on a legal form for your business is keeping you up at night, we recommend two effective solutions. First, go eat another chocolate bar. (You could drink more wine or take another bath, but we know what we'd do.) Second, remember that your business structure is not carved in stone. If you decide later that you don't like it, you can change it.

Licensed to Fill

We're talking about filling work orders, of course. What kind of licensing will you need to operate in the staffing services industry?

The answer is, "It depends." In most states, all you need are the usual business licenses (e.g., city, state, county). But some states have required specialized licenses in the past, and laws do change. Be sure to check your own state's laws.

Generally, the staffing industry has not required licensing. Industry experts say that, in part, this is because staffing services don't charge fees to people who sign up with them. In contrast, some employment agencies do charge such fees.

Risky Business

Proper insurance coverage is a must in this industry. "If you don't control that from day one, you're just dead," says Rita Zoller.

The "Business Insurance" chapter in *Start-Up Basics* covers the subject in detail. Following are the types of insurance that are most relevant to the staffing services industry:

- *Errors and omissions insurance.* Also known as professional liability insurance, this type of policy protects your staffing service when you, your staff, or your employee allegedly makes an error or omission that causes financial loss to your client's company. Defending yourself in court can be costly, so make sure your policy covers defense expenses in addition to the limits of liability. This is better than lumping defense costs and award payments together under the liability limits. Also, make sure your policy is offered on an occurrence, rather than a claims-made, basis. Otherwise, if the client waits to make the claim, you may not be covered even if the loss occurred during the policy period.

  Errors and omissions insurance is especially important and sometimes essential in health industries. Malpractice insurance for doctors or lawyers should be carried by the temporary worker or covered by the client.

- *Fidelity bond.* You'll need a fidelity bond to protect you if an employee steals client property or forges a time sheet. Equally, you'll want protection if an employee steals from you. An additional consideration is that bonding adds respectability to a business and increases client confidence. You may have heard that bonding is not, strictly speaking,

> **Smart Tip** *Tip...*
>
> Having complete records of employees' work assignment dates, assignment cancellations, etc., can help you keep your insurance costs down. For example, staffing services can more easily fight—and win—unjustified unemployment claims when they have everything documented in the computer.

▲

insurance. However, this is only partly correct. Some types of bonding are not insurance because you have to pay back the bonding company. Fidelity bonds, however, are insurance. Following are the three types of coverage:

1. *Individual bonds.* These cover each employee separately.

2. *Schedule bonds.* Employees are covered according to their positions in your company. Greater responsibilities require a greater bonding amount.

What's Your IQ?

No, not that IQ. We're talking about your insurance quotient. Adequately protecting your business is a complicated undertaking. Make sure you have the following bases covered:

○ *Consider every aspect of replacing items.* When everything in one staffing service owner's office was stolen a year after she opened for business, her insurance replaced equipment at a higher level than the original equipment. This was great. Unfortunately, she hadn't considered the consultants necessary for setting up the new equipment. Her staffing service had to pay consulting fees (about $7,000) all over again.

○ *Consult your insurance company about special coverage.* A client company once wanted to send one of Patricia Troy-Brooks' New Castle, Delaware, temporary employees to Colorado for a few months. What, you may ask, is the problem with that? The plane could go down or the employee might get hurt in Colorado. In unique cases like this, be sure to phone your insurance company. In Troy-Brooks' case, she had to get a special rider.

○ *Develop company procedures to minimize your risk.* The following are all good practices:

– Get a thorough and accurate job description for every employee you place. Make sure the receptionist you send out on an assignment doesn't have duties that include carrying 50-pound mail bins to the loading dock every night.

– Stay in close communication with temporary workers to see if there are changes in job descriptions.

– Make sure you have the appropriate disclaimers on the backs of time sheets (see Chapter 10).

– Have employees sign their time sheets to indicate that all information is correct and that they did not sustain any injuries on the job.

These strategies may help prevent you from making insurance-related mistakes that end up costing you big bucks.

3. *Blanket bonds.* These cover all your employees together.

Every owner we spoke to had bonding. You should get a broad form fidelity bond, because, unlike a standard fidelity bond, it extends coverage to clients' property (rather than covering only your own). It also covers defense costs. Although general liability insurance usually provides defense coverage for lawsuits arising from mistakes or negligence, it doesn't cover any fraudulent or dishonest act.

Your client list and your list of temporary employees are both vitally important pieces of property. If an employee steals them, you could suffer a serious financial setback. Make sure these items are covered by your bonding insurance.

> **Smart Tip** Tip...
>
> When you apply for insurance, make sure your application includes all the types of services you provide. Then carefully review all the exclusions of the policy to make sure no aspect of your business will be left uncovered. If you can't get coverage for some part of your business, don't give up. The insurance market does change. Keep checking back periodically.

- *General liability insurance.* This insurance will protect your company against accidents and injury that might occur at a work site or at your office. You may be liable for bodily injuries to customers, guests, delivery people, and other outsiders—even when you have exercised "reasonable care."

  The staffing industry has several special needs with regard to this type of insurance. Make sure your policy covers off-site employees. It is also good to have coverage for clients' property or equipment that is under the care of your employee.

  The standard amount of liability insurance to carry is $1 million.

- *Unemployment insurance.* You need insurance to cover unemployment claims. A staffing service may get a handful of claims each week.

- *Workers' compensation insurance.* You are liable for your employees' injuries caused by on-site equipment problems or poor working conditions. State law requires you to insure your company against potential claims of this type. However, the amount of employee coverage and the extent of employer liability depend on individual states' laws.

If you've been working along with this book, you now have a business plan and have completed many of the legalities necessary for starting your business. (See? That wasn't so bad, was it?) So it's time to get down to money matters. This is what we will focus on in Chapter 4.

Show Me the Money
Financing Your Business

Before you spend too much time worrying about how to finance your new staffing service, you should first figure out how much start-up capital you'll need and what your operating costs will be. In this chapter, we'll show you how to do that. Then we'll outline your financing options.

Cranking It Up

The staffing industry has higher start-up costs than do many other industries—for a couple of reasons. As we mentioned earlier, a home office is not usually a reasonable option. (You don't want all those people traipsing through your house, do you?) Also, you'll have to meet payroll immediately, even though your business may have no income for a couple of months.

This said, how much money will you need to get your staffing service up and running? Some experts suggest that you double the amount of money you think you might need. We'll take both a general and a specific look at start-up costs. First we'll cover the factors that help determine start-up costs, and we'll examine the costs of two hypothetical staffing services. Then we'll provide you with real-life detail by letting you read start-up stories from some staffing service owners and fill out a start-up worksheet with your own data.

The Gist of It

Your start-up costs will depend greatly on the following factors:

- *Size.* Obviously, starting out with a small office and few permanent employees costs less than starting out with a larger facility and numerous permanent employees.

- *Niche.* Some sectors of the industry are more expensive to operate in than are others. As a rule of thumb, the more highly skilled the job assignments your company handles, the higher your start-up costs will be. There are at least three reasons for this: (1) employee salaries will be higher, (2) the need for a certain image may require a more expensive location, and (3) computer demands (both hardware and software) for testing and training will be greater. The most expensive niche in which to start up appears to be the medical staffing industry (see Chapter 1).

- *Geographical location.* Office rent, employee pay, advertising costs, tax rates, and insurance rates all depend on both your area of the country and the city/town distinction.

To help you figure your own costs, take a look at the start-up expenses for two hypothetical staffing companies on page 47.

The staffing service at the low end of the industry does light industrial and low-end clerical work. Its office is located in an industrial area and occupies 800 square feet. It has a small training and testing room with two computers. The owner handles the recruiting and bookkeeping himself. He employs a sales manager and a receptionist/coordinator. Gross annual sales are $500,000.

The staffing company on the high end places employees in high-end positions in the computer industry. The office is in an upscale downtown location. It covers 2,200 square feet and has a large testing and training center with a network of 10 professionally installed computers. The owner places some of the temporary employees herself. She employs a sales manager, a recruiter/coordinator, a receptionist, and a payroll/administration officer. The company expects to reach $1 million in gross sales.

> **Beware!**
> Dyana Veigele of Seattle's Law Dawgs feels that starting up a staffing service shouldn't be attempted on a shoestring. "I wouldn't recommend anybody doing it," she says, "without either a good loan, a credit line, or capital."

Note that the suggested operating capital is relatively high for both of these companies. This is because you must pay your temporary employees before you receive payment from clients.

Getting Real

Here is a sampling of some owners' start-up experiences:

George Sotos started as an executive recruiter in Chicago, launching his first company in 1999. He conducted high-level talent searches that took months to complete. Seeking a more regular revenue stream, he decided to expand into the temporary placement market. "I wanted to set up more of a store," he says. Using his proceeds, he bought one temp firm in 2001 and another in 2002, then combined all three.

Now George has six full-time employees filling job orders. Operating out of two offices, one in downtown Chicago and one in the suburbs, his firm primarily handles office and clerical workers. The work is demanding and the hours are long, but George is happy. In fact, he's still looking to buy more firms and merge them into his growing operation.

Indianapolis-based Rita Zoller and her daughter spent about $7,000 of the $20,000 they had on start-up costs. "We [already] had a desk and a phone and a computer, but no industry-specific software," says Zoller. So they invested in software, advertising, and insurance. "If you wanted to start up right," she adds, "it would cost you a whole lot more. We actually started in my kitchen and moved into an office two months later." They were able to start without an office because their

> **Smart Tip**
> If you decide to get a bank loan, look for a banker with whom you can establish an effective financial relationship. You should expect and receive good service. Do not be afraid to negotiate with your banker. Remember that as your business grows and becomes profitable, you can often renegotiate loan terms.

first job was a payroll account that they handled without hiring employees.

The biggest start-up expenses for their company, First Call Temporary Services, were for advertising, industry-specific software, and insurance. Making payroll was not a big problem because they negotiated immediate payment of invoices.

Patricia Troy-Brooks of Advanced Staffing in New Castle, Delaware, started with $75,000. She had two desks, a phone, borrowed furniture, and

Bright Idea

When seeking start-up capital, don't forget to look at the certificates of deposit, mutual funds, and other investments you hold. Sometimes these can be cashed in for funding.

Alternate Route

The staffing industry is well served by companies that provide a wide range of financing options to help owners meet accounts receivable. This is a function, among others, of factoring and funding companies.

Factoring companies usually specialize in providing working capital, although some bigger companies offer capital for other uses. In general, factoring companies buy invoices. They then handle client billing and collections. Their fee, called a "factors fee," ranges anywhere from 1 percent to 5 percent of the invoice amount, depending on the company's pricing structure. If your client is late in paying, the factoring company assesses you interest (usually about 1 percent per month) until the bill is paid. If your company grows large quickly, you may decide to use this type of service.

Funding companies can lend you the money you need to meet your payroll or expand your company. They also lend money for use as working capital or to cover personal needs. Larger staffing services use funding companies to finance acquisitions or franchise buyouts. In addition to lending money, funding companies can offer your business back-office support (e.g., handle your payroll). "I don't see, unless you're independently wealthy, how anyone can do it without a funding company," says Patricia Troy-Brooks. "I can tell you, when we won [one particular] contract, they owed us $1 million before they paid us one dime." Costs vary widely, depending on the services you choose, but typically you'll pay a percentage of your gross sales. One owner says that at first she paid 5 percent, but she has negotiated that number down.

These types of companies advertise in trade journals (see this book's Appendix for a good start). If you use them, you'll probably be able to hire fewer permanent staff members.

three months' free rent. Like other owners we spoke to, she estimates that computers and software were among her biggest expenses. Advertising, additional office equipment, and payroll for her permanent employees were other significant expenses. She had no direct payroll expenses for temporary employees because she used a funding company to pay them (see "Alternate Route" on page 46 for a discussion of such companies).

Now it's time for you to estimate what your own costs will be (see the worksheet on page 49). So go to it!

Revving Up

We've discussed your "outgo." What about the income you can expect?

Gross revenues from privately owned staffing services vary widely, anywhere from about $400,000 for a very small service to $15 million for a service with several offices and upwards of 35 permanent employees. Industry expert Mike Ban estimates that the average privately owned staffing service has gross revenues somewhere in the neighborhood of $750,000.

Start-Up Expenses

	Low	High
Rent/deposit	$1,500	$4,000
Equipment and supplies	6,000	20,000
Software	2,000	8,000
Payroll (temporary employees)	36,000	68,000
Insurance (first quarter)	1,700	2,400
Phone and utilities	200	400
Payroll (permanent employees)	4,600	10,800
Owner salary	3,000	4,200
Advertising/promotion	1,400	3,000
Licenses and taxes	270	350
Professional fees	400	4,750
Misc. (business forms, postage, signage, etc.)	380	600
Total Start-Up Costs:	*$57,450*	*$126,500*
Suggested operating capital:	$80,000	$135,000

Full Throttle

Several owners said it was difficult to know when their staffing companies first produced a profit, because revenue went toward buying more equipment, paying off loans, or hiring more temporary employees. But First Call Temporary Services produced a profit in four months. "We were really fortunate," Zoller says. Advanced Staffing and PDQ Personnel Services (in Los Angeles) were both profitable by the end of the first year.

Smart Tip

How, you may ask, did Advanced Staffing's Patricia Troy-Brooks manage to get three months of free rent? She learned from a mentor who taught her that if you don't ask, you don't get anything. "They can only say no," Troy-Brooks points out.

According to industry experts, it is reasonable to expect your staffing service to make a profit some time within the first two years.

Money Matters

By now you've probably decided that you'll need more money than you have to launch your business. So where are you going to get your start-up funds? The "Getting Financing" chapter in *Start-Up Basics* covers this topic in detail, but we will take a quick look at your options for financing your staffing service start-up.

Straight to the Source

Following are some of the most common choices in the staffing industry for finding financing. Most of the owners we spoke to used a combination of sources to provide their funding.

- *Yourself.* Your own capital is the best source of financing. It is immediately available, with no interest accruing and no obligations. Dyana Veigele and her husband never took out a loan. They started small. Rita Zoller and her daughter started First Call with $20,000 of their own money from an IRA.
- *Friend or relative.* This is another good option, although no owners we talked to reported using it.
- *Silent partner.* One owner started with the financial help of a silent partner (i.e., a partner who had no role in running the company) who lent her $150,000 in return for a share of company profits.
- *SBA.* To cope with their rapidly expanding business, Zoller and her daughter took out an SBA loan.
- *Bank.* Patricia Troy-Brooks started Advanced Staffing with a $75,000 bank loan. Besides offering loans, banks also offer lines of credit to established

businesses. Continued growth prompted Zoller and her daughter to decide to get a line of credit from a bank.

- *Funding company.* Funding companies lend money for a variety of purposes, including payroll, working capital, and expansion. They also offer back-office support.
- *Factoring company.* This type of company buys invoices (manages receivables) and handles invoicing and collections.
- *Equity.* If you have equity, you can use it to get a bank loan. In Los Angeles, PDQ owner Patty DeDominic used her house as collateral.

Start-Up Expenses Worksheet

	Start-Up	First Six Months	Total Cost
Rent/deposit			
Equipment and supplies			
Software			
Payroll (temporary employees)			
Insurance (first quarter)			
Phone and utilities			
Payroll (permanent employees)			
Advertising/promotion			
Licenses and taxes			
Professional fees			
Misc. (postage, signage, etc.)			
Total Required			

Here comes the easy part. Working horizontally, add "Start-Up" figures to "First Six Months" figures to produce "Total Cost" figures. Then work vertically, adding "Total Cost" figures to come up with a "Total Required" figure. This is the amount you'll need to start your business and keep it going for six months.

- *Credit card.* This is a last-resort financing option. Interest rates are very high. None of the owners we interviewed reported using this method.

Once you have your money, it's time to start recruiting the help you'll need to get your business going. This is the topic of the next chapter.

5

The Staff Dreams Are Made Of

In this chapter, you'll learn about the permanent and temporary employees you'll need to run your business. We'll also discuss effective ways to recruit workers, what to look for in your employees, and how to test and screen applicants for your temporary work force.

Employing the Best

Employees are what the staffing industry is all about, so you will want to make sure you get good ones. In this section, we will show you how to do that. The employees you will need fall into two categories: permanent staff and temporary employees.

Here to Stay

There are many different tasks to be covered at a staffing service. If you are starting out small, you'll perform many of those tasks yourself. For the positions we list below, note the variety in titles and in the duties assigned to each position. Both the assignment of titles and the division of labor are handled differently from service to service, so our list is only approximate and very general in nature.

With those caveats in mind, take a look at the permanent positions typically found in staffing services.

- *Administrative assistant.* This employee provides assistance to upper management.
- *Administrative coordinator.* This individual handles payroll, billing, and accounts receivable. In a smaller service, he or she may also handle the purchase of supplies and be in charge of weekly mailings.
- *Bookkeeper/financial services manager/payroll representative.* The person in this position deals with payroll, both internal (i.e., permanent staff) and external (i.e., temporary workers). The same person may also do collections and billing. Many larger staffing services employ several of these individuals in their finance division.
- *Corporate administrator.* This individual handles purchasing and provides human resources support for permanent staff.
- *Office manager/branch manager.* This employee oversees all office operations. Staffing services with more than one office usually have one office manager at each location.
- *On-site coordinator.* This person oversees temporary employees at the work site. This position is usually only necessary when there are large groups of temporary employees at a single site, e.g., workers at a factory.
- *Permanent placement specialist.* This individual handles recruiting, interviewing, selection, and placement of permanent employees for the staffing service's clients.

Bright Idea

Do you have a family member you can hire? The staffing industry has a long tradition of family-run businesses. In fact, two owners with whom we spoke started their staffing services with their daughters, and were extremely pleased with the results. A family member with whom you get along well could add a lot to your business.

- *Placement specialist/performance supervisor/personnel coordinator/employment counselor.* This employee handles initial calls from prospective temporary employees. He or she also interviews applicants, supervises temporary employees, and deals with any employee-related problems a client may have. All staffing services of any size employ several of these individuals at each office location. Even

> **Smart Tip**
>
> Make sure all your firm's applications require candidates to state how they discovered your company. This will provide you with valuable information for your recruitment tracking.

a small service usually has at least two people handling these tasks. However, in a small office, these individuals may also be recruiters.

- *Receptionist/secretary.* This person answers phones and handles office tasks.
- *Recruiter.* This employee finds and interviews applicants and may also provide customer service. Most sizable staffing services have several of these individuals at each location. In a small service, the recruiter and the personnel coordinator may be the same person.
- *Risk control officer.* This person handles all insurance needs for the staffing service. Many services can and do successfully handle their insurance needs through an outside insurance agent. However, very large staffing services, as well as services in sectors with high personal injury risks (e.g., the industrial sector), often have in-house risk control officers.
- *Sales manager/sales associate.* This individual handles sales and is usually out of the office generating business. He or she also provides customer service. All but the very smallest staffing services usually have at least two of these positions at each office location.
- *Regional director/vice president of operations.* This person oversees company operations. If there is more than one office, then the regional director supervises the office (or branch) managers.

Now that we've gone over the types of positions most staffing services have, let us stress that most privately owned start-up services have very few permanent staff members. So don't shake your head in despair, wondering how the heck you're going to come up with all these employees. Instead, read on as we discuss which of these positions you absolutely must have covered.

In New Castle, Delaware, Patricia Troy-Brooks, owner of Advanced Staffing, estimates that you need a minimum of two people when you start out: one to get clients (i.e., a sales associate), and the other to find and supervise employees (i.e., a recruiter/coordinator). "From there, you add your front-desk person," says Troy-Brooks. Until you have that person, your recruiter/coordinator will also be answering phones. Note that your sales associate will not be able to do this because he or she will be out of the office most of the day.

Several of the owners we interviewed started out with only two people (themselves and one other person), adding more as their businesses grew. You can do the same. Several years down the road, you may have a dozen or more permanent employees. In the next few paragraphs, we briefly outline the personnel situations of some of the owners we interviewed.

Advanced Staffing works mostly within the office and clerical sector and has 23 permanent staff members divided between the company's two offices. Troy-Brooks has five people in her finance division. She also has a regional director, a branch manager, and several sales staff members. Nearly half of her permanent employees are devoted to recruiting and training the temporary staff.

In Seattle, Dyana Veigele's Law Dawgs has five permanent employees, including herself and her husband. She is the attorney, recruiter, and president of the firm. Her assistant is director of placement. They have two other placement people. Veigele's husband, who has an MBA, handles the business and technical aspects of running the company. They have no payroll people because they outsource that function.

Rita Zoller's First Call Temporary Services operates primarily in the industrial sector with 35 permanent staff members spread among four offices. Each office has several personnel coordinators, a receptionist, several recruiters, some sales staff, and an office manager. Zoller also has on-site coordinators, one comptroller (i.e., chief accountant), an individual to handle her accounts payable and receivable, and a risk control officer.

Once you are ready to hire employees, what should you look for? Skills and experience are important, of course, but they are not the only considerations. Don't forget personal qualities. Personality is important in any work situation, and the staffing industry is an especially people-oriented business. Also remember that making good personnel choices the first time around is important, because the hiring process is expensive.

That said, you should look for the following personality traits:

Stat Fact
According to one Harvard Business School study, companies often do a poor job of judging a candidate's motivational and cultural fit. Corporate culture can include anything from dress code to office regulations. Mismatches in motivational and cultural fit account for 80 percent of today's performance-related turnover.

Smart Tip
There is no substitute for learning all you can about the recruiting business. After all, you cannot conquer a problem without knowledge. Read all the articles, books, and journals you can find. In addition, the American Staffing Association offers a variety of resource materials. (See the Appendix for information.)

- *Unflappability.* Your staff, particularly "frontline" employees like personnel coordinators and recruiters, must be able to deal effectively with stress. When trouble strikes, these people have to be able to handle the stress.

- *Multitasking ability.* With phones ringing all morning and many tasks to be completed in a narrow time frame, you need staff members who can handle more than one task at a time. "If a person does not know how to multitask and handle multiple priorities, they likely will not do well in this industry," says Patricia Troy-Brooks.

> **Bright Idea**
>
> Don't forget less conventional means of recruiting. You could hire a skywriter to fly over a beach with your ad at spring break time. Set up a tent, provide soft drinks, and let students fill out applications while they cool off in the shade.

- *Ability to get along with others.* In a small company, conflict is very obvious. Hard as it may be, don't be afraid to let employees go if they don't fit in with the rest of the office. Conflict interferes with morale and productivity.

- *Ambition.* This industry is highly competitive and demanding. You need employees who enjoy being challenged.

OK, you say. Those are all great personality traits. But how do I know who has them?

Good question. How do you judge what you're getting in a prospective permanent employee, someone you don't even know? To maximize your chances of ending up with employees who provide the best possible fit for their positions and for your company, consider the following strategies:

- *Provide a thorough, solid description of the position.* List the requirements of the position and the skills and qualities you are looking for in the successful candidate. This point sounds obvious and easy, but many firms don't do it effectively.

- *Give behavioral interviews.* Here, the questions focus not only on candidates' competencies, but also on their cultural and motivational fit with your staffing service. For example, questions such as "How would you handle X situation?" can be effective.

- *Give candidates projects to do together.* That way you can observe how they work, perhaps as part of the interview process.

- *Use a valid personality assessment.* This tool can help you understand candidates' real strengths and weaknesses. Psychological tests like these are readily available through bookstores and business schools. For more on interviewing, read the "Employees, Benefits, and Policies" chapter in *Start-Up Basics.*

We've shown you what to look for in your permanent staff, so now let's focus on one of the most crucial aspects of your business: your temporary employees.

Hired Hands

The type of temporary workers you'll look for depends, quite obviously, on the kind of staffing service you decide to operate. For example, if you specialize in legal work, you'll be looking for attorneys, law clerks, etc. If you focus on clerical placements, you'll look for administrative assistants, data entry keyers, and other office personnel.

How many temporary employees should you have? This is a difficult question. You need enough employees to provide you with a profit, but not so many that you can't pay them while you wait for clients to pay you. Furthermore, the number of temporary employees you need depends on how much profit you make from your employees' labor. Your profit margin, in turn, depends on the employee pay rate and your markup rate. All of this means that, as with so many aspects of this business, the number of temporary employees you should hire depends in large part on which industry sector you are working in.

If we lost you there, don't worry. We'll have more to say on all of these points in Chapter 9. But let's get a ballpark idea of one section by looking at the number of temporary employees that several of our sources have on their rosters. All three of these owners place workers in mid- to high-end office and clerical positions, and all three also place in other industries such as the technical sector.

One owner has nine permanent staff members and a lineup of 200 to 300 temporary workers. Another has 23 permanent staffers and about 500 temporary workers. The third has 34 permanent employees and 800 to 900 temps. All these figures for temporary workers include not only those employees who work fairly continuously during a given period, but also those who work more occasionally.

If you do the math (temporary workers divided by permanent workers), these staffing services have between 21 and 33 temporary workers for every permanent employee. This is an inexact method, of course, because the number of staff members dealing directly with temporary workers varies from service to service. But you get the idea. If you start out with two permanent staff members (including yourself)

> ### ⚠ Beware!
> Although there are many personality profiles available, it is essential that you select one that is valid, reliable, and nondiscriminatory. If you hire an assessment firm, make sure that it supplies validation data and a written guarantee that you will be held harmless if a lawsuit results from the use of its assessment tools.

> ### Bright Idea
> Consider doing, on a smaller scale, what one large staffing firm did. It set up interactive computer kiosks on college campuses. In so doing so, they were able to screen out a lot of people. Targeting bright, motivated people and making it easy for them to sign up is really smart.

and are working in the office and clerical sector, a roster of approximately 50 temporary workers is probably realistic.

In Chapter 2, we covered some of the things to look for in temporary employees, including the right paperwork (proof of citizenship or legal resident status), test scores that indicate good skills, and a sat-

Bright Idea
Some staffing services have been known to offer $50 signing bonuses to new employees. This strategy might help you recruit for hard-to-fill positions.

isfactory interview. These are all good indicators. But remember that appearance, personal habits, and the ability to communicate say something important about an applicant's inner qualities. Look for the candidate who arrives on time (assuming you have scheduled a test or interview), dresses appropriately, and communicates well. In addition, look for evidence of common sense in temporary employees. Lack of common sense is a frequent employer complaint about temporary employees.

The Recruiting Challenge

The number-one challenge for the staffing industry remains this: how to find and hire the workers you need. The strategies we suggest hold true for the recruitment of permanent staff as well as temporary employees, although emphasis will be placed on the latter. For more detailed information on recruiting, see the "Employees, Benefits, and Policies" chapter in *Start-Up Basics*.

The Problem

We touched on the recruitment problem earlier. To recap, recruitment is a problem even in a time of relatively high unemployment because the recent recession has made employers skittish about taking on new workers. Companies have also gotten pickier about whom they will hire. Meanwhile, the traditional work force is shrinking, in part because the oldest baby boomers are reaching retirement age. All these trends together yield a shortage in skilled labor. That is why so many companies turn to staffing firms to provide needed personnel. In fact, surveys by various groups, from the Conference Board to the Center on Policy Initiatives, show that 90 to 95 percent of businesses turn to staffing companies for

Smart Tip
One way to maximize your chances of retaining your temporary employees (a topic we'll cover in the next chapter) is to hire reliable workers in the first place. One rule of thumb: 80 percent of your problems will come from 20 percent of your temps. Check references and employment records well.

temporary help. In addition to seeking skilled labor, companies also turn to staffing firms for work-force flexibility. In a recent survey by the WE. Upjohn Institute for Employment Research, 52 percent of the companies cited unexpected increases in business as the most important reason for using temp firms. Some 47 percent said they did so to fill temporary vacancies, 47 percent did so to replace absent regular employees, and 36 percent did so to get help with special projects.

> **Bright Idea**
>
> Age before beauty. Retirees are increasingly available, and senior citizens make reliable employees. Your company can attract retirees by putting job notices up at local offices of the American Association of Retired Persons and the National Council on Aging.

So whether economic times are tough or not, temporary services are still much in demand. Even when there is no apparent labor shortage, companies still find it difficult to locate the right candidates for open positions. This creates a constant need for you to recruit the kinds of workers your clients want.

Don't lose heart; recruitment is not an unsolvable problem. Even during labor shortages, such as in the mid- to late '90s, good employees could be found. Remember that unemployment rates only tell part of the story. The statistics used for calculating unemployment percentages only count people who are actively seeking work and collecting unemployment benefits from their state. The designation "unemployed" doesn't cover any of the following people:

- New college grads
- Displaced homemakers (those returning to the work force after raising children)
- Immigrants
- People working full time but seeking additional work
- People working part time but seeking additional work
- Retirees looking for supplemental income
- People trying to change careers

As the list demonstrates, even a low unemployment rate does not mean that no one is looking for work. Many people are. Thanks to its flexibility, the staffing industry is uniquely positioned to take advantage of these groups' availability.

A shrinking pool of traditional candidates is not an insurmountable barrier, either. "Traditional candidates" has historically

> **Bright Idea**
>
> Staffing pros get first crack at graduating students by sitting on advisory boards at local universities and community colleges. To attract laid-off executives, employees give talks on career management at meetings of associations such as the American Society of Certified Public Accountants.

meant white males. Businesses, including staffing services, are now working harder to adjust to a more diverse work force.

So if these are all difficulties that can be overcome, why is recruiting such a thorny problem for client companies and staffing services alike? How exactly can we overcome the recruiting problem? Read on.

The Solution

"What?" you ask. "There's only one solution?"

That's right. Work harder.

"Thanks a lot," you reply. "That's really helpful."

OK, maybe we should rephrase that a bit. Work harder at recruiting. And work smarter. What does that mean? All of the following:

- Make recruitment a top priority. You'll need to put time, thought, energy, and creativity into it.
- Offer your employees the maximum flexibility.
- Offer employee training.
- Offer expanded benefits and competitive salaries.

Looking in All the Right Places

There are many ways to find employees. Some means are more creative than others. You should try for a good mix of the methods we discuss below.

Referrals

Studies show referral is the most effective (i.e., least expensive and most productive) way to recruit employees. Some staffing companies receive as many as 40 percent of their new hires from referrals. In Indianapolis, Rita Zoller estimates that referrals comprise about 36 percent of her applicants. She estimates that she places about 70 percent of all applicants.

"I would say referrals are where we have the greatest success," agrees Patricia Troy-Brooks. Another company asks every applicant to provide five names of people who might be interested in working for them.

Smart Tip

Tip...

Concentrate your recruiting efforts where they'll be the most effective, and make sure you know where they are likely to be the least effective. For example, if your staffing service works at the higher end of the office and clerical sector, you probably won't place many executives. Your clients will turn to the many executive search firms that place high-level candidates.

▲

Every owner we interviewed has given employees, both permanent and temporary, bonuses for successful referrals.

Try to get referrals from the following people:

- *Clients.* This may seem like a strange source. However, sometimes clients know who they would like to see in a position, but they aren't able to offer that person a permanent job.

- *Employees.* Those you hire may know others who are looking. Offer referral bonuses for successful hires.

- *Applicants.* These people are also likely to know others who are job hunting. Be sure to include a referral question on all application forms.

Beware!

The bigger your employee pool, the better your chances of being able to consistently fill work orders (i.e., have a good "fill rate"). However, you do not want to get a reputation among workers as a service that does not provide its employees with enough work. Make sure you monitor where jobs are coming from and what skills are needed. Use this information to guide your recruiting efforts.

Talking It Up

To be effective, any recruiting brochure you put together should make clear the many advantages of temporary work. Make sure your brochure mentions the following important benefits that temporary work provides:

○ The opportunity to sample and compare different industries and different companies in those industries

○ A chance to try out many different companies without having to go through the tedious hiring procedure (applications, interviews) at each company

○ The "inside track" to job opportunities in a company

○ The crucial "foot in the door" and the chance to become known at a company

○ A "beefed up" resume

○ The chance to brush up on important skills

○ Financial stability during a search for permanent employment

○ An improved self-image

The inclusion of these important points in a brochure with an attractive photo can go a long way toward helping you recruit the temporary employees you need.

- *Receptionists for companies you call.* Receptionists often get calls and unsolicited resumes from job seekers. Companies who prefer to do their supplementary hiring through staffing services may be willing to give you names and phone numbers.
- *Job-training professionals.* Build relationships with public and private job training programs. Program leaders are typically eager to help students find jobs. You could also offer incentives.
- *Other staffing companies.* Sometimes job seekers call your service about positions in an industry you do not handle. A staffing service that places workers in a different industry sector than you do might be willing to enter into a reciprocal agreement with you, whereby you each refer such "lost" candidates to the other.

Advertisements

- *Newspaper.* This is a good method if you need lots of people quickly or very broad-based skills. Consider ads in smaller daily or weekly newspapers. Make sure the ad describes the job and the skills needed to perform it. Rita Zoller finds that major newspapers are effective for finding light industrial or clerical workers. "We do not advertise in the paper for our professionals or IT," she says.
- *Specialty publications.* These include neighborhood monthlies, arts listings, and religious or business publications. All of these can be effective for targeting particular groups. Several of the owners we talked to advertise this way.
- *Business cards.* Carry business cards with you wherever you go. You never know when the person sitting next to you might be a good prospect.
- *Yellow Pages.* A good old-fashioned Yellow Pages advertisement remains useful for recruiting. Dyana Veigele finds that their ad pays for itself. Take a look at the sample Yellow Pages ad below:

New Millennium Staffing Inc.

HIRING DAILY!

◆ Vacation Pay   ◆ Free Software Training

◆ Medical Insurance   ◆ Flexible Hours

◆ Top Wages Paid Weekly ◆ Part- and Full-time Work

oo Century Blvd.
Normal, IL 61761
(ooo) 345-5555

- *Television.* Consider cable TV, which is less expensive and easier to localize. Recruiting experts in the staffing industry consider cable TV an effective option.

- *Radio.* In theory, this could be an effective means of targeting a particular location and type of candidate. However, most owners have had no success with radio. Responses they did get suggest that it might work better for targeting clients, but overall, it doesn't seem to be a productive means of advertising for this industry.

Beware!

If credit ratings are used to exclude an applicant, federal law requires you to notify the applicant so they have the opportunity to correct the record. Also, the use of credit reports may be discriminatory, which could cause equal opportunity problems.

- *Internet.* For staffing services in certain industry sectors, especially professional and technical, effective recruiting is achieved by searching resume databases or by posting job openings on a job listing database. Maintaining a Web site is also an effective way to collect resumes.

    The Internet is also a good recruiting tool for the professional, clerical, and IT sectors.

- *Fliers, posters, newsletters, and brochures.* Visually appealing printed material that you pass out or post in strategic locations can also work well.

    Free self-paced software training is a powerful recruiting tool. You can advertise this benefit heavily on fliers around town, especially at the unemployment office.

    When Dyana Veigele started her first business in San Diego, she and her partner used fliers to get the word out. "My partner was a male, and during [law school] breaks, we would go in the bathrooms and put our fliers in the stalls. And then we'd start getting calls, and that's how we started," she says. Don't forget to put your recruiting fliers where they'll really count: at various centers of influence. These include other businesses, your local chamber of commerce, churches, civic clubs, colleges and other institutions of higher learning, community centers, credit unions, employment offices, health spas, military recruiting offices, placement offices, real estate agencies, and Welcome Wagon organizations.

- *Trade journals.* These are most effective for recruiting in professional and technical industry sectors.

Promotions

- *Site banner.* Consider putting up, with your client's permission, a banner at the job site (e.g., a factory). This works best for recruiting large numbers of temporary employees to work at the same site.

Dressed for Success

Clothes make the worker. Consider setting up a wardrobe closet for employees who lack the business wardrobe necessary for making a professional appearance on the job. The closet might include dresses, blouses, suits, and shoes for women, as well as shirts, slacks, ties, suits, and shoes for men. How do you assemble such a closet? You might start with donations from yourself and your permanent staff members. Or try talking to a local clothing store or chain. Perhaps store executives will donate items or sell them at nominal cost.

Patricia Troy-Brooks of Advanced Staffing came up with this idea years ago. She hit upon it when she started her own career because she had too little money with a wardrobe that was too casual for the business world. "When you don't feel on a par with your peers," she says, "you're intimidated." Ultimately, that affects performance because self-esteem is low, which can hinder career growth.

- *Job fair.* You could hold one as well as attend others. Job fairs are particularly good for finding highly skilled candidates. A recruiter for the technical division of one business hits all the high-tech job fairs.
- *Open house.* A well-advertised open house at your staffing service could be a good recruiting tool. As a community event, it would even qualify for free publicity in the newspaper.

Part of the recruiting challenge is learning to do it cheaper and more effectively. The first step is to track the source of your employees. This sounds very simple, but many companies fail to do adequate tracking. As we have seen, possible sources of temporary employees include the following:

- *Referrals* (friends, family, co-workers, etc.)
- *Advertisements* (newspaper, TV, radio, Internet, etc.)
- *Promotions* (job fairs, trade shows, etc.)

Make sure all prospective employees state on their applications how they found your service. Try to elicit information that is as specific as possible. Then go through the applications and sort them according to source. Once you have your statistics, ask yourself the following questions:

- *What is the cost per applicant from each source?* For example, if your Yellow Pages ad costs you $300 per month and you have about 15 applicants a month who say they found you through the Yellow Pages, this means each applicant from that source cost you $20. If you found 24 applicants through referrals, and any bonuses you pay only apply when applicants pan out (see Chapter 6 about employee referral bonuses), then each referral applicant has cost you $0 so far.

- *What percentage of applicants comes from each source?* If, as a monthly average, you get 60 applicants (using the numbers above), then 25 percent of them came from the Yellow Pages and 40 percent came from referrals.

- *What percentage of applicants from each source are put to work?* Let's say you end up hiring three of the Yellow Pages applicants. This means that 20 percent of your Yellow Pages applicants were successful. On the other hand, if you hired 16 of your 24 referral candidates, your success rate was about 67 percent.

- *What is the cost per new employee from each source?* Your three new Yellow Pages applicants cost you $100 each. (You could argue that the Yellow Pages are also used to gain clients, and therefore the true cost for recruiting is not the full $300 per month. However, because owners say the Yellow Pages are not effective for finding clients in this industry, we assess the full cost of that advertising to recruiting.)

If we assume that all the referral candidates were found by employees and that you give bonuses for successful employee referrals, then each of the 24 new employees cost you anywhere from $25 to $50, depending on the size of the bonus. More realistically, some of these referrals probably came to you free, reducing the per-employee cost to something more like $20 to $40.

It is clear to see that referrals are much more cost-effective than your $100-per-head Yellow Pages ad. Which is not to say you should cancel that ad immediately. It may be a reasonable cost compared with other advertising methods. You won't know until you take a look at the performance of all your sources.

You don't have to do anything fancy to track the success of your recruiting sources. Unless you have a big staffing service, you can even do your tracking by hand. Gather all your data, wait for a slower month (you'll have one sooner or later) and then sit down with a calculator, a nice sharp pencil, and a good cup of coffee. Once you've finished, you'll have a much better idea of how effective each of your recruiting efforts has been.

Testing and Screening Your Employees

In this section, we will discuss different ways to test and screen your temporary employees. Note that these methods can also be used to evaluate your permanent employees.

As we noted earlier, staffing services use both written and computerized tests. Increasingly, however, the latter are winning out. The speed and accuracy of scoring as well as ease of administration make a good case for using computerized testing whenever possible.

An in-depth discussion of testing software can be found in Chapter 7. For now, we'll provide a quick run-down on the software used by the owners we interviewed, and then we'll move on to list other types of testing and screening that you may want to consider.

Rita Zoller tests prospective employees on general and clerical skills using SkillCheck. For some, Prove It! and Qwiz testing software do a good job.

Owners can tap more than 200 different tests, ranging from clerical to computer use to accounting tests. Patty DeDominic of Los Angeles' PDQ Personnel Services uses PreValuate. In addition, her company teamed up with California Community College to produce a test that measures not only reading, math, and clerical skills but also logic and judgment. Law Dawgs has developed some of its own software, tailored to the legal sector.

Temporary and staffing companies are responsible for their employees, just like any other company. Make sure you consider the following testing and screening processes, where they are warranted:

- *Employment application.* This should be detailed, or it should be accompanied by a detailed resume. Look for unexplained gaps in employment history or a declining salary history. Make sure you get written authorization for verification of all information and indicate that false statements are grounds for immediate dismissal.

- *Interview.* As we have mentioned, behavioral interviews that include "What would you do in this situation?" questions can be effective in getting below the surface.

- *Reference check.* This one seems too obvious to mention, but many employers fail to check the references cited on candidates' applications. At the very minimum, check the previous employer. Get applicants to sign legal forms releasing previous employers from liability for providing a reference. Also, ask former employers specific questions about the candidate's past behavior (absenteeism, improper conduct, etc). For legal reasons, many employers will refuse to answer these questions, but it doesn't hurt to try.

- *Educational records check.* It is surprising how many applicants make false educational claims, especially considering how easy these records are to check. A candidate's educational background provides good clues about qualifications and motivation level.

- *Honesty tests.* These are relatively new and quite promising. They are also widely available, cost-effective, time-efficient, and accurate. Need we say more? You can acquire these and other psychological testing materials from bookstores and business schools.

Stat Fact

One major corporation recently found that 80 percent of the candidates it tested for support staff positions failed the basic tests and could not be hired.

- *Graphoanalysis.* This is also known as handwriting analysis. It is gaining popularity, but there is widespread disagreement regarding its effectiveness. And there is a big problem with finding truly qualified examiners.

- *Drug screening.* Some of your clients may require all employees you send them to be screened for drug use. When conducted by professionals, such screening is relatively inexpensive and almost 100 percent accurate. However, research your state's laws regarding testing procedures because several states have restricted this screening device. Also, provide for backup testing in cases of positive test results. This way, you can avoid discriminatory practices.

- *Criminal history check.* Failure to obtain, or attempt to obtain, criminal history data is the single most common reason for employer liability. If you place someone with a criminal record who then starts embezzling money from your client, you could be found guilty of negligent hiring. To be found not guilty, you must prove that you did not know, and could not be expected to have known, about the employee's background. Criminal history information can be obtained easily in most states.

- *Credit check.* Credit reports contain much useful information, including the names of previous employers. However, they are also frequently inaccurate and perhaps more trouble than they are worth.

- *Motor vehicle records check.* This screening device is imperative for any position involving driving.

- *Investigative agencies.* Hiring an agency is only worthwhile if you have a lot at stake. The cost varies. The litigation risk can be shared, although many agencies include a disclaimer.

Now that we've taken a look at the various testing and screening devices, how should you use them in operating your business?

You should take the following steps:

- Determine what kind of check is needed.

- Look at all applications closely.

Beware!

Keep in mind that although there are quite a few different computer software testing programs on the market, applicants may have taken the exact same test at other staffing services, or at least have taken other tests that are similar.

Smart Tip

Make sure you are aware of any screening needs particular to your chosen industry sector. For example, conflict of interest checks are common in the legal staffing sector. "Large-case litigation is prevalent here, and we have to do conflict checks to make sure people haven't worked on the opposing side," says Dyana Veigele. This, she adds, holds true for everyone from attorneys down to secretaries.

- Call or write for references.
- Decide whether you need to check for criminal records or other information. If you have doubts, delay hiring until your checks are completed.
- When an employee changes jobs, reconsider the level of background checking necessary.

For more on screening potential employees, check out the "Employees, Benefits, and Policies" chapter in *Start-Up Basics*.

We hope the information in this chapter will help you find employees, test them, and screen those who pass the tests. Most of all, we hope that you develop a staff of terrific employees who will help your staffing service thrive.

6

Making the Grade
Retaining Your Employees

Keeping your employees once you have them is another thorny problem in the staffing services industry. This chapter provides you with ideas about how to do that. We will also discuss employee training, pay rates, benefits, and appreciation, all of which are key retention issues. Finally, you will learn how to evaluate your employees.

Finders, Keepers

The difficulty in retaining temporary employees (i.e., external staff) gets most of the press. This is understandable because the labor and expertise of your temporary work force are the products you are selling. No product, no company—it's that simple. And it's perfectly true that not only are other staffing companies competing with you for these all-important temporary employees, but so are companies in general. Many of your carefully screened, painstakingly trained personnel will leave your service to accept permanent positions. "I would say that 10 to 15 percent of all our placements end up in permanent placements," says Dyana Veigele, owner of Seattle's Law Dawgs. The American Staffing Association has estimated that up to 40 percent of all temporary employees are offered full-time jobs at their company assignments.

So it's easy to see why retention is a problem that will—as it probably should—keep you up at night from time to time. And why we're covering the topic in some detail.

Less often discussed is the problem of keeping your permanent employees (i.e., internal staff) from walking out the door. It's a high-turnover industry for internal staff. Burnout is common because staffers work long hours under high stress. And, as we have seen in previous chapters, the nature of the business demands multitasking, which is tiring and intense.

So how do you keep your employees, both temporary and permanent, with you for the long haul?

There are numerous strategies you can use to keep employees interested in working for you. Offer training, pay employees well, provide attractive benefits, and offer a variety of bonuses and incentives. We will discuss all of these strategies below.

Spring (also Summer, Fall, and Winter) Training

Although training is usually discussed in reference to temporary employees, you should offer skills enhancement to all your workers. Training is increasingly important in the staffing services industry, especially in more specialized areas. What form does this training take? It depends on the nature of the skills needed. For administrative and clerical people, it could range from training in word processing and spreadsheets to fairly advanced training in computer sciences. There's even a company that places temporary pilots and trains and qualifies these pilots for various grades of aircraft.

Patricia Troy-Brooks, who owns Advanced Staffing in New Castle, Delaware, believes strongly in the value of training. "We do specialized training for our customers where we offer to prepare employees and help them transition into the organization and reduce the learning curve," she says. Offering training to your temporary workers not only helps retain them, but also makes good business sense. After all, a more skilled worker commands a higher pay rate. The higher the pay, the greater your own profit. But what about permanent employees? Are there benefits, beyond the retention issue, to providing them with training?

You bet. The staffing services industry continues to change rapidly, and your staff members need to stay abreast of these changes. New technology, new selling techniques, changes in employment laws, and the huge impact of the Internet are all compelling reasons to keep your permanent employees in the loop.

Following are some ways to provide your employees with training. Most of these methods are both economical and effective.

- *Computerized training.* You've invested in computers and a variety of software packages; now make sure they get good use! Every employee can benefit from added computer skills. This type of training is suitable for all your workers.

- *Videotapes, audiotapes, books, articles, and pamphlets.* The ASA offers a variety of all these to its members. Your local library may also have useful resources. Try setting up a small library for your employees. Some videotapes are ideal for use in group orientation of new temporary employees. All these types of materials are suitable for both permanent and temporary employees.

- *Mentoring programs.* These can be informal (e.g., within your own company) or more formal (e.g., involving local businesses, universities, or colleges). This method is most suitable for permanent employees.

- *Invited speakers.* Local businesses and institutions of higher learning are rich sources

Bright Idea

Sometimes temporary employees in the professional sector have additional rounds of interviews with client companies before winning a job assignment. Dyana Veigele's legal staffing service provides these employees with interview training in the form of role-playing.

Smart Tip

Successful staffing companies invest in a lot of training software to teach employees how to handle particular aspects of the jobs they'll be assigned to. To cover all the bases, training efforts shouldn't stop there. You can give employees a handbook, show a video, and present required reading. Extra time in orientation pays off later!

of potential speakers. Often, retirees are happy to come and talk about their professions. Check clubs and other organizations for possible speakers. This training method is probably most suitable for permanent employees.

- *Outside seminars and classes.* Community college tuition is usually inexpensive. Look into seminars and classes your employees could take. This training method could be offered as an elected benefit (e.g., instead of vacation time) to either permanent or temporary employees.

Paid in Full

In addition to offering training, staffing firms can retain good employees by offering attractive pay rates and salaries. Keep as close to the top of the pay range (see "Sample Pay Rates" below and on the next page) as you can manage.

What you pay your employees, both office and field staff, will depend on the following factors:

- *Employee skills.* Salaries and pay rates are consistent with the skill level of the work performed. A registered nurse makes more than a receptionist. And in "hot" segments of the industry, like information technology or the professional sector, skilled workers are receiving top dollar for their services.

- *Amount of experience.* A worker with several years of experience in a position earns more than someone just entering that position.

- *Supply and demand.* Salaries rise in a labor shortage. Of course, you will "pass on" the cost of field staff to your clients, adding a markup percentage. Therefore, high employee earnings are good news for your staffing service.

   In addition, some locations have particularly high demand for specific types of workers. This factor also increases pay rates. "Legal secretaries are always in demand, says Dyana Veigele, "but we're seeing an increase in paralegals. They bill time and bring in revenue, and may be used in lieu of attorneys."

- *Geographical location.* The higher the cost of living, the higher employees' salaries will be. Generally, the Northeast (especially New York City) and the West Coast (especially California) have higher pay scales. Similarly, workers in cities earn more than those in small towns.

Beware!
Even if your client is unhappy with an employee's work and refuses to pay you (or you decline to accept payment) for that employee, keep in mind that you are legally responsible for paying all employees who are where they're supposed to be when they're supposed to be there. Note, however, that you are not obligated to send that worker to any other assignments.

- *Worker seniority.* A good employee who has been with your service for at least six months deserves to receive better pay than someone you have just hired. Also, senior staff often get first crack at higher-paying assignments.
- *Negotiating ability.* Both your own powers of negotiation (with clients) and your employees' ability to negotiate (with you) may affect what you pay employees. A worker with valuable skills in a hard-to-fill job area may be worth the sacrifice of some of your own "cut," especially if the client making the work order request is a valued client.

> **Smart Tip** Tip...
>
> In some cases, keeping talented employees means paying them even when they're not working. It's called "benching." If a service doesn't have an assignment for them to start that day, they're paid anyway, so that they won't jump ship. This expensive strategy should only apply to workers with unique skills whose assignments provide you with an excellent profit.

Below, we provided pay ranges for the permanent employees that staffing owners typically hire (see Chapter 5 for an explanation of each position's responsibilities). Remember that the factors we just discussed all affect pay levels. This accounts for the broad range in salaries and hourly rates.

It is important to realize that these figures are base pay figures. They do not include bonuses, which can add a large percentage to an employee's paycheck.

Sample Pay Rates—Permanent Staff

Position	Pay Range
Administrative assistant	$8–$12/hr.
Administrative coordinator	$21,000–$27,000
Bookkeeper/financial services manager/payroll representative	$22,000–$30,000
Corporate administrator	$22,000–$30,000
Office manager/branch manager	$29,000–$51,000
On-site manager	$26,000–$54,000
Permanent placement recruiter	$24,000–$70,000
Customer service rep	$24,000–$38,000
Receptionist/secretary	$7–$15/hr.
Sales rep	$24,000–$50,000
Regional director/vice president of operations	$30,000–$50,000

Sample Pay Rates—Temporary Staff

Position	Pay Range
Administrative assistant	$8–$12/hr.
Attorney	$25–$150/hr.
Bookkeeper	$9–$13/hr.
Computer programmer	$35,000–$55,000
Data entry operator	$7–$9/hr.
General office assistant	$7–$9/hr.
Graphic designer	$11–$22/hr.
Help desk support (computers)	$22–$26/hr.
Office clerk	$6–$9/hr.
Mailroom clerk	$7–$12/hr.
Paralegal/law clerk	$10–$25/hr.
Picking/packing operator	$7–$9/hr.
Receptionist	$7–$15/hr.
Secretary	$11–$20/hr.
Systems analyst (Microsoft-certified)	$25–$50/hr.
Shipping/receiving operator	$8–$12/hr.
Web site builder	$20–$50/hr.
Word processor	$14–$27/hr.

The table above shows pay ranges for some temporary positions frequently handled by staffing services. Again, they are wide ranges, for the same reasons cited above. All are day-shift rates. (Night-shift rates are usually higher.)

Added Benefits

The benefits you provide your employees can go a long way toward helping you retain workers. After all, temporary staffers want, and deserve, the same kinds of benefits as people with permanent jobs. In fact, ASA surveys show that 74 percent of temporary employees take temporary assignments as a way to get permanent positions.

All owners indicated that their temporary workers had to be employed for a certain length of time (usually a few months) before they became eligible for company-subsidized benefits.

Benefits you should consider providing include the following:

- *Health insurance.* Most owners we interviewed provide some kind of health insurance, although the amount of subsidy varies.
- *Life insurance.* This is one of the less common benefits, but it's offered by some companies.
- *Paid vacations and holidays.* All owners we talked with offer this benefit, at least once the temporary employee has worked a certain number of hours or days.
- *Pension plan.* Except for the very large staffing services, few staffing firms offer pension plans or 401(k) plans. Some

Smart Tip

Even with a long vesting period (waiting period before temporary employees become eligible), providing benefits like health insurance and a 401(k) plan can give you a significant advantage in retaining employees, especially in very competitive sectors. "It's nice to have those things, even if they are never used," points out Rita Zoller in Indianapolis.

Tip...

owners are working on 401(k) plans but don't yet have them in place. Remember that participation laws require you to provide similar benefits for all workers. This means that if you provide your permanent employees with a 401(k) plan, you must also provide a 401(k) plan for your temporary employees.

- *Tuition reimbursement.* As training becomes increasingly important, more and more staffing services may consider it worthwhile to pay for, or contribute

Farming It Out

One way to provide benefits for your employees is to get someone else to do it for you. So to speak.

As we mentioned in Chapter 1, professional employer organizations (PEOs) usually take over the human resources functions of a client company, leasing that client's employees back to the company. One of the human resources functions PEOs can provide is benefits management.

Most PEOs have predominantly small businesses as clients. This is because small companies have the most to gain from the use of a PEO. Depending on the types of services you choose to buy, a PEO can save your company from having to undertake the expense of setting up a human resources department and a payroll department. And it gives your employees access to better benefits than they would have otherwise, because a PEO can take advantage of economies of scale and buy benefits more economically than you can as a single small company. It's a legitimate way for a company to be able to upgrade the benefits it can provide to its own employees.

toward, their employees' continuing education. Few of the owners we talked to provide this benefit yet.

For an in-depth discussion of benefits, read the "Employees, Benefits, and Policies" chapter in *Start-Up Basics*.

Just Rewards

The staffing industry is one that lends itself particularly well to a merit-based pay system, especially for permanent employees. Everyone we talked to offered some kinds of bonuses to both temporary and permanent workers. Most offered permanent employees the chance to significantly enhance their base pay rates via a variety of bonuses. Here are some of the typical bonuses awarded in the industry.

- *Acceptance bonus.* If your service needs a worker for an especially hard-to-fill position offered by a valuable client, it may be reasonable to offer a bonus to the employee who takes the position. Depending on how important the client is, and therefore how desperate you are, this bonus would be paid instead of, or in addition to, a higher hourly rate.

- *Performance bonus.* This incentive is common in the industry. Several owners we interviewed reward good work this way. This type of bonus could apply to both permanent and temporary employees, although it is more frequently given to the former. It is usually handled as a percentage of the base pay rate.

- *Referral bonus.* All owners that were questioned for this book said that they have given bonuses to both permanent and temporary staff for the referral of qualified applicants.

Asset Appreciation

Your employees are your greatest asset. Every business owner knows you're supposed to show your staff that you appreciate their good work. But hectic schedules and pressure-filled lifestyles often get in the way. Nevertheless, it's easy enough, if you try, to find chances to thank your permanent staff.

Bright Idea

For many people, group benefits are an extremely desirable advantage, even if they have to pay the premiums themselves. Law Dawgs offers short-term benefits that are available to employees, unsubsidized, upon placement. Then, after an employee works 1,500 hours, the company subsidizes medical, dental, and vision insurance at 50 percent.

Bright Idea

Want your temporary workers to show up for work every day in each new assignment? Offer them a bonus for perfect attendance. That's what Rita Zoller does, to great effect. She recognizes that each of her temps is an ambassador for her company.

But what about your temporary employees? That's right. What about the people whose expertise and labor you're selling? In this industry, it is easy to forget that they, too, are your employees, rather than merely a product or a commodity. Part of the problem is that you never see them working, because they do that on clients' premises. In fact, you may never see them at all once they've signed on with your service. It's possible that the only contact you'll have with many of your employees will be over the phone. Yet it is important to treat employees well and make them want to come back.

Bright Idea

Make sure your employees, both permanent and temporary, know you appreciate them. One way to celebrate your shared endeavor is to hold an open house party at your office. This could be over the holidays or, better yet, during the week in October that the United States Congress has declared "National Staffing Employees Week."

The Empathy Factor

Put yourself in the place of a temporary employee. Although meeting new people and experiencing new work situations can be exhilarating, it is also stressful. Think about the "first days" you've experienced on the job. Every temporary employee ends up with a whole lot of these.

In an ideal world, the company contact would meet the employee with a broad smile and a "Welcome aboard," introduce that employee around, explain everything that needs to be done, and generally make the employee feel right at home. The reality usually falls far short of this ideal, however. Recognize that your temporary employees have a whole host of minor annoyances to deal with, such as not knowing where anything is. Familiarity with one's co-workers, the office layout, and many small details is something full-time workers tend to take for granted but that a temporary employee lacks.

Recognizing this fact, Rita Zoller encourages temporary employees to drop by to pick up their paychecks on Fridays. She views this as a good opportunity to thank them for working all week. Often her office provides cookies or candy. "Keep it personal, and let them know that they're appreciated," she advises, "because they may not be shown that by clients." Of course, she admits that the personal touch is more difficult in a bigger city, where you have to deliver checks. "The most important thing you can do is just treat people with respect," she adds.

Anything you can do to make your temporary employees feel at home when they come into your office will be appreciated and will probably increase retention rates.

> ## Smart Tip
> *Tip...*
>
> Permanent employees
> have a lot of information
> about how your company oper-
> ates and who your clients and
> temporary employees are. Your
> employee contracts should
> include a noncompete clause,
> which says that staff members
> cannot start up their own
> staffing businesses (or go work
> for another staffing service)
> within a certain specified geo-
> graphical radius and within a
> specified period of time.

One good way to show appreciation and consideration for employees is to keep them working. If an employee's assignment ends sooner than scheduled, make every effort to place that employee again right away. People count on making a given amount of money, and a temporary employee's income is already less certain than are most people's incomes.

The tip boxes in this chapter provide additional ideas for making contact with your temporary employees and for making them feel valued. Chances are, the effort you make to show appreciation to your temporary employees will result in higher morale and higher retention rates.

Making a List and Checking It Twice

Evaluation of your employees is an important part of your business. Although your particular evaluation strategies will depend on whether the employee is permanent or temporary, some general principles apply in each case. Make sure you do the following:

- *Develop minimum performance standards.* This means making clear to the employee the expectations for the position. Some of this can be handled in orientation.

- *Provide feedback.* Feedback is the second most powerful known motivator. Permanent employees should be given some feedback before the performance review. Because you are not on the job with your temporary employees, feedback will have to wait until you get a performance review (i.e., evaluation) from the client.

- *Review performance.* For permanent employees, this means answering questions like those on page 79. For temporary employees, the evaluation forms you receive from clients will form the basis of the performance review.

For your permanent employees, a competency-based performance review is important. The following five questions

> ## Smart Tip
> *Tip...*
>
> Don't bother sending out
> general satisfaction sur-
> veys to your customers, as used to
> be the industry norm. Although
> these surveys sound like a good
> idea, most clients are too busy to
> complete them. Besides, if they
> have a problem with one of your
> temps, you'll hear about it soon
> enough. "Bad news travels fast,"
> says Rita Zoller.

are particularly appropriate for the staffing services industry:

1. How competent is the employee technically (e.g., on the computer)?
2. How capably does the employee handle clients?
3. How good are the employee's people skills?
4. How innovative is the employee?
5. Does the employee demonstrate integrity?

Beware!

One poor evaluation should not cause you to drop an employee from your roster. Two, however, especially if they happen back to back, should make you reconsider calling that temp again. It doesn't make good business sense to call a person who receives poor evaluations.

The last question is as important as the others because the review should focus not only on the results achieved, but also on the manner in which the employee achieved those results.

The performance review for temporary employees consists of evaluations received from clients. At the end of an assignment, call the supervisor to request an evaluation of the employee's performance. Try to get an evaluation in writing and to get different kinds of information about the employee. We provide a sample evaluation form on page 80.

- *Provide (more) feedback.* This will be round-two feedback for your permanent employees. For your temporary employees, keep in mind that what you pass on from the evaluation your client provides may be the only feedback your employee receives. On-the-job feedback may be completely nonexistent.

- *Link financial compensation to performance review.* No company is so small that it can't link the bonuses that permanent employees make to the quality of their work. Performance bonuses are the way to do it. For temporary employees, opportunities for creating a link between money and performance are less obvious, but you certainly should not give a raise to an employee who isn't doing a good job. (In fact, you should stop placing that employee, even in a tight labor market.)

Smart Tip

Client contracts should contain a "no hiring" clause. This says that the client can't hire a temporary employee you sent them on assignment unless they either pay you a fee or wait anywhere from six months to a year, depending on the agreement. This clause protects you from losing employees you have spent time and money recruiting, testing, and often training.

We have focused our attention here on employee evaluation. Also consider having temporary employees evaluate both your

Sample Evaluation Form

New Millennium Staffing Inc.
oo Century Blvd. • Normal, IL 61761
Phone: (000) 345-5555 • Fax: (000) 234-5555

Please rate (e.g., poor, fair, good, excellent) the performance of the employee named below.

Employee_____

Position_____ Date(s) worked_____

Rating

Personal appearance   _____

Attendance   _____

Team player   _____

Organizational ability   _____

Reliability   _____

Technical skills   _____

Comments:_____

_____

_____

_____

_____

_____

Signature_____

Company _____ Date _____

Thank you very much for providing this information.

staffing company and the client companies where they work. A few questions and a rating scale are all you need to cull information that will be useful both to you and your clients. This information could be provided anonymously.

Now that you have some employees, it's time to set up your office and buy equipment. In the next chapter, we turn our attention to these tasks.

7

Home and Hearth
Equipping Your Business

You and most of your permanent staff will spend a lot of time at the office. You need working space that is comfortable and unimposing, yet also encourages productivity and professional conduct. The right layout, as well as an appropriate choice of furniture and equipment, can help you achieve these goals. In addition, a good choice of professionals to work with you can help you protect your assets.

In this chapter, we'll discuss the important space-related elements of a staffing office. We'll also go over the equipment you'll need. Finally, we'll tell you about the professionals whose services you'll find valuable.

Laying It Out

What should your staffing service office look like? Your goal should be a setting that is both professional and welcoming. In this section, we'll take a look at making the most of the space you have.

We divide the following space features into two groups: crucial and optional. The latter are areas that are desirable and should be considered only if you have the space.

Crucial Areas

- *Reception area.* As with any business, this area should be right near the entrance. It should be as spacious as you can make it. Several owners mentioned the usefulness of a long, divided counter so that several candidates can fill out applications at once. Large, open reception areas help to foster a friendly feeling.

- *Testing and training center.* All owners we talked to had an area set aside for testing and training.

> **Bright Idea**
> When you become more established, consider having an office built for your company. Rita Zoller did, and she loves it. "That office is perfect," she says. "Everyone should build their office if they're in the temporary [help] business." Her office even has sliding glass doors to an outside patio!

Larger staffing services sometimes separate these and have a facility for each. Even in a small office, you should set aside some space for this function, including a training area with multiple workstations that temporary employees can use between assignments.

- *Office.* You need at least one office where you can conduct interviews. At First Call Temporary Services in Indianapolis, most offices have doors, and even workers in cubicles have access to offices when needed. In an interview situation, privacy should be maintained as much as possible.

- *Staff office.* Computer workstations for your permanent staff can be housed in this room. Ideally, front-office tasks (e.g., matching temporary employees with work orders) are conducted in separate facilities from back-office tasks (e.g., payroll).

Optional Areas

- *Conference room.* This is useful for holding staff meetings. It also aids occasional client meetings, if you don't want to use your office.

- *Offices.* You will find uses for any extra offices you can supply. They may become secretarial suites, sales areas, customer service offices, or coordinator offices. "The coordinators have to talk to each other so much that we have windows cut out between all their offices," says First Call's owner, Rita Zoller. "But you can slide them shut or leave them open." These windows are one of her favorite features.

- *Management offices.* Members of management often have private offices.

> **Smart Tip** Tip...
>
> Don't forget the personal touch. Flowers (high-quality silk ones are your best bet), framed prints or drawings, photographs (perhaps job-related), and other items of décor can add important touches to your office.

Spaced Out

What about space? You can start up with as little as 700 square feet, as long as you are prepared to expand when you need to. Owners we interviewed had start-up space ranging from 700 to 1,500 square feet and now have company offices ranging from 2,000 to 10,000 square feet.

Good Stuff

This section will give an overview of the general equipment and office supplies in which staffing service owners typically invest. Then we will cover computers and industry-specific software, each in a separate section, because these are particularly important for accomplishing the tasks required of a staffing company. Finally, we will discuss Internet services.

Talking Generalities

The types of equipment you will need will vary depending on the demands of your business. However, there are several basic pieces of equipment that most new business owners need. Following is a list of equipment that you should have:

- *Office furniture.* You'll need filing cabinets and bookshelves. You'll also need desks and chairs for yourself and your permanent staff, as well as for computer stations. However, as long as you provide a few separated testing booths, you could get by with a long table, on which you could put several computers for training purposes. Plan your office layout (see "Laying It Out" on page 84) before you make decisions about furniture. High-quality used furniture is an option, as long as it is in good condition. You need to present a professional image.

- *Phone.* A good phone system is important in this business, most of which is conducted via telephone. You may be able to get by with two phone lines when you start out, but expect to have to add more before long. Make sure any phone system you invest in is easy to operate. You don't want new personnel hanging up on clients or temporary employees while trying to transfer their calls or put them on hold. You should have a professional-sounding promotional message that plays while callers are on hold.

- *Answering machine.* This is a must for collecting messages after hours. Invest in a quality one.

- *Cellular phone.* Today, a cellular phone is a must-have for any business owner. And in a staffing service, sales personnel will benefit from them because they spend so much time out of the office.

- *Fax machine.* All owners we spoke to have fax machines. You will need one, too. Consider buying a top-of-the-line fax machine; it will get a lot of use.

- *Copier.* This is another item that will receive use, for everything from the copying of various business forms to the production of fliers. You should invest in at least a midrange one.

- *Scanner.* Some staffing services have scanners. Whether you invest in one may depend not only on the size of your service but also on the industry sector you'll be working in. Scanners are useful for inputting resumes into your computer, among other purposes.

The right equipment is important to the success of your staffing service. Once you have purchased it, make sure you insure your equipment for replacement cost rather than the original cost, which can be significantly lower.

Stocking Up

In addition to the usual office supplies (e.g., stationery, employee applications, etc.), you'll need to keep all of the following industry-specific supplies on hand:

- *Orientation handouts.* You should have some printed material to give new temporary employees. See Chapter 2 for samples.

- *Test forms.* If you use pencil-and-paper tests, you will need to keep these in stock (plus the pencils!).

- *Time sheets.* Unless you use time-and-attendance software (see "The Softer Side" on page 87) that produces computerized work records, your temporary employees will use these to note their hours worked for a client. You will use your copy of their time sheets to prepare invoices.

Booting Up—Computers and Related Hardware

The staffing services industry depends heavily on computer technology. Expect to spend a significant portion of your start-up money on computer systems and the hardware and software for running them.

Smart Tip Tip...

You will probably need to pay extra for insurance to cover the cost of computer installation, in addition to the cost of the computers themselves. This is worthwhile, however, because computer consultants are expensive.

- *Computer.* Even if you start very small, you'll need two computers, one for office use and one for testing and training. Without a printer, a basic computer system will cost anywhere from $1,500 to $3,500. To use the software necessary in this industry, you'll need 128 to 256MB RAM. You should have a hard drive with at least 40GB of memory. Make sure your computers have drives to play and perhaps record on CDs or DVDs and that you have backup capability for preserving your precious business records.

- *Internet connection.* You'll need reliable high-speed links to the Internet, for downloading files (e.g., resumes, work orders) and using e-mail. Many businesses use a cable modem provided by the cable company or DSL (digital subscriber line) provided by the phone company, depending on local availability.

- *Printer.* You may only need one printer, but it needs to be a quality one. Letters you send clients, as well as any other printed material your office produces, should look professional, which means you need a laser printer.

The Softer Side

Operating in most sectors of the staffing industry will require you to buy a lot of software. What do we mean by "a lot?" That depends on the niche you choose. In general, the better the skills of the temps you place and the more computer-oriented your niche is, the more software you can expect to buy.

Software packages have broad price ranges that depend on the method of sale, the number of users, and the amount of technical support required. Some packages are sold by the workstation. Others are priced based on a monthly subscription per user. Still others are handled by a license (a document permitting a specified number of users) that represents either an outright sale or a yearly fee.

A complete front- and back-office staffing package (not including testing and training software) for one workstation typically costs anywhere from $1,000 to $3,000 (or even \$4,000). Monthly subscription rates also vary greatly, usually costing between \$50 and \$250 per month per user for a front- and back-office package. Licenses vary so greatly in cost that any range we provide would be too wide to be informative.

In many cases, you can also buy individual pieces of software. If you need only a few items (e.g., a couple of tests), this is the way to go. On the other hand, if you need quite a few, you'll probably save money by buying a package. Because individual pieces of software vary so greatly in complexity and therefore in cost, a price range would be meaningless. As an example, however, you can expect to buy most individual tests you might need for \$100 to \$600.

Now that you have some of the scoop on software, let's take a look at what you might need. (See the Appendix for a listing of software suppliers.) Staffing services use computer software to perform the following tasks:

- *Applicant and employee tracking.* Keeping good records of applicants and temporary employees involves a lot of data. Industry-specific software packages allow you to input resumes, edit those resumes, and record information including history, work interests, interview responses, test scores, and assignment history. Most also allow you to view several records simultaneously, integrate information with e-mail and fax software, customize searches, and generate reports. Complete Office Automation for Temporary and Staffing Services (COATS), MAESTRO Staffing Management System, and TempWorks are some of the software packages that help with these tasks.

- *Employee monitoring.* If you send large numbers of workers to the same location, you can install an electronic keypad at the client's location and track employees' attendance via modem with Time and Attendance Command Center (TACC) Software.

- *Payroll/accounts and payable/accounts receivable.* To accomplish these back-office tasks, you must produce paychecks, reports, invoices, letters, and statements; figure out deductions; update invoices and accounts, and complete a whole host of other tasks. Fortunately, there are plenty of industry-specific products to help you. Back-office software packages like

> **Smart Tip**
>
> If you don't already have the computers you're planning to use, wait to buy them until you figure out which software you'll need. That way you'll be assured of having adequate hardware with which to run your programs.

> **Bright Idea**
>
> Often, software demo disks or downloads are available so that you can try out a company's product before you buy. In addition, many software packages come with guarantees (e.g., a 30-day money-back guarantee).

eEmpACT, MAESTRO Staffing Management System, and TempWorks handle all these concerns, in addition to others.

> **Smart Tip** — *Tip...*
>
> Don't forget that sometimes you can negotiate a more favorable price for software, especially if you are buying a lot of it.

- *Placement.* Typical placement tasks require access to data like employee availability status, pay and bill rates, assignment start and end dates, skill codes, employee performance notes, number of employees needed, etc. Representative software packages that have placement functions include COATS, Maestro Staffing Management System, and myTTrax.

- *Recruiting.* You'll want software that can help you recruit from the Internet as well as keep track of your other recruiting sources. Both eEmpACT and myTTrax software packages can be used for recruiting, among other purposes.

- *Sales.* You will need to keep track of a lot of client-related information, too. Most software packages allow you to sort clients into categories, create letters, conduct direct mailings, and access client history, among other tasks. Representative software packages that help you handle sales include COATS, TempWorks, and myTTrax.

- *Testing.* Your temporary employees must be skill-tested before you can place them. The available testing software covers every imaginable skill area. Rita Zoller recommends SkillCheck for new owners because it is good and relatively inexpensive. Other owners are happy with Prove It! and Pre-Valuate. Or you can have software custom made for your business, as Patty DeDominic did. Available testing software includes Prove It!, Qwiz, SkillCheck, and Pre-Valuate.

- *Training.* Some of the testing software also has training applications. Qwiz and SkillCheck can help to train employees.

Surfing the Net

The Internet is increasingly important in the staffing services industry, not only for recruiting temporary employees, but also for finding clients. Every owner we talked to has access to the Internet.

Your degree of success in recruiting candidates will depend on your level of expertise with the Internet and on the amount of time you have to surf Web sites. You can recruit employees by using three types of sites:

1. *Job posting databases.* For a fee, you can list your job opening on a job posting database. Advantage: Candidates who don't want to post their resume may find you. Disadvantage: So might everyone else, such that you'll end up sifting through many unsuitable resumes. A list of job posting databases appears in this book's Appendix.

2. *Resume posting databases.* Also for a fee (usually applied to each applicant record you request), you can search for applicants who look promising. Advantage: This method is much less time-consuming than sifting through tons of resumes. Disadvantage: You may get unreliable information because resumes are not screened. You can end up wasting time and money on unqualified applicants. See the Appendix for a list of resume posting databases.

3. *Direct company postings.* Every staffing service owner we spoke to has a Web site and uses it for recruiting purposes. Many allow candidates to apply directly through the Web site. You will probably find that your staffing service needs a Web site, even if you operate in sectors other than the technical and professional sectors of the industry. Web sites can receive several thousand hits every month, with steadily growing traffic.

> **Beware!**
> Having an amateurish, hard-to-navigate Web site is not a good way to attract candidates or clients. Get a professional to help you design and maintain your site. Make sure your Web site is worded so that it can be "matched" by search engines like Yahoo! It is also important to keep your site up to date.

Your Web site is also a good place to advertise and attract potential clients. Make sure you have an attractive site that is easy to navigate.

The cost of operating a Web site depends on who designs and maintains it for you. If you hire a professional to do it, costs range anywhere from $50 per month for maintenance to $600 per month for a wider range of services.

While the Internet has been received with hostility by some staffing professionals, others welcome it and note that its advent has not diminished the need for staffing companies. Although the uncensored nature of the Internet may be refreshing, the information on it is also largely unverified. Staffing professionals are uniquely positioned to establish their reputations as bastions of informational integrity in online recruiting.

For more on the Internet, read the "Starting an E-Commerce Web Site" chapter in *Start-Up Basics*.

Adding It Up

Use the checklist on page 92 to estimate what your equipment needs will be. Your office and the equipment in it make important contributions to your staffing service's efficiency and productivity. The professionals with whom you consult also have crucial contributions to make. We'll examine these in the last section of this chapter.

Professional Edge

Most of the professionals you'll need to consult are the same ones any business owner needs. The difference will be in the industry-related concerns you have. Following are some of the individuals you may need to help you with your staffing service:

- *Accountant.* You may not have your own in-house bookkeeper right away. In this case, you'll need an accountant, and preferably one who is familiar with the staffing services industry. Ask other staffing service owners in your area for recommendations. Because a good accountant can do much to further the success

---

High-Tech Trends

More and more, new advances in software are changing the way staffing services conduct their business. Here are some tasks that may be affected by changes in technology.

○ *Placement.* Most software packages have the ability to generate availability lists (aka "hot lists") easily. Some even generate "probably available" lists, allowing the staffing company to reduce gaps between assignments.

More and more staffing services and their clients communicate online. Available software makes it easy to download work orders and input them into a database. This may mean less time on the phone and quicker, more efficient matching.

○ *Interviewing.* Quite a few software programs allow staffing companies to conduct interviews online and create a record of the interviewer's impressions and the candidate's interpersonal skills. This can be useful for a first interview, especially if the candidate is in a remote location.

○ *Payroll.* Most staffing services use signed time sheets to record a temporary employee's hours for the payroll division. If you have the right software and a large number of employees at the same site, you can install an electronic keypad at the client's location and keep track of employees' hours via modem. This method eliminates difficulties like trying to read handwriting on a time sheet and trying to get employees to turn in time sheets promptly. Eventually, technological advances may mean that even those who are the only temporary worker at a site can log in their hours electronically.

There are many tasks that are much easier and more efficiently accomplished than they were a decade or so ago. Expect even more changes in the future.

---

of your business, don't be afraid to interview candidates to find the best one for your business. You can find out more in the "Bookkeeping," "Financial Statements," "Financial Management," and "Taxes" chapters of *Start-Up Basics*.

- *Attorney.* A good lawyer is important in this industry. You'll likely want a large law firm with many departments because you'll need attorneys to redo leases, work on employment issues, or tackle workers' compensation problems. Of course, retaining

> **Bright Idea**
>
> Some staffing services have begun setting up online referral groups whose members all serve the same industry sectors. If a staffing firm does not have a qualified candidate to fill a work order, they query other group members until they find a good match for the client's needs. Then they present the other company's candidate to the employer and split the fee.

a good attorney can be expensive—but in the long run, well worth it. Some staffing owners also rely on their attorneys for business consulting.

- *Banker.* Cash flow is a frequent problem in this industry. Good banking relationships are crucial. Try to find a banker who is familiar with the challenges of running a staffing company. If you hire a funding company or a factoring company (see Chapter 4), personnel from these institutions will help you to ensure the financial stability of your staffing service.

- *Computer consultant.* You will need professionals to set up all your computer workstations. You will also need them to install the software you buy and to train you and your staff in its use. Often, software packages come with a certain number of consulting hours built into the price. However, you will probably have to pay extra to get in-depth training. Computer consultant fees generally range anywhere from $125 to $400 per hour, depending on how specialized the

Equipment Checklist

- ❏ Office furniture
- ❏ Phone
- ❏ Phone line(s)
- ❏ Message system
- ❏ Cellular phone
- ❏ Computer
- ❏ Printer
- ❏ Scanner
- ❏ Software (front and back office)
- ❏ Software (testing and evaluation)
- ❏ E-mail/Internet access
- ❏ Fax machine
- ❏ Copier
- ❏ Office supplies
- ❏ Miscellaneous

services are that you need. These fees do not include travel, lodging, and meals for out-of-town consultants.

- *Insurance broker.* Choose your insurance (and also your broker) carefully; adequate coverage is especially important in this industry. Larger companies may hire a permanent employee to handle risk control. You won't need one until your staffing service gets larger, and you may not even need one then. But you need an insurance agent who will be responsive and who will provide you with good service. Some insurance companies specialize in policies for the staffing services industry. For more on insurance brokers, see the "Business Insurance" chapter in *Start-Up Basics.*

- *Staffing consultant.* Whether you are just starting up or are expanding your business, this individual can be a great help.

- *Webmaster.* Trendy name aside, this is an important professional to have on board because your Web site needs to be well-designed and maintained. If you don't stay up to date, you may lose out to rivals. Maintaining a site is fairly costly, but more owners agree that the benefits outweigh the costs.

Getting the Job Done
Attracting and Keeping Clients

The first part of this chapter title pretty much answers the second part. In other words, if you provide employees who get the job done and do it well, then clients will find you, and they will stay with you. What we offer in this chapter are some additional ways to get the word out about your staffing service, as well as ways to ensure that this word is a complimentary one. We will discuss advertising, networking, honing your image, and delivering good customer service.

Madison Avenue

Traditional advertising can be effective in the staffing services industry, as long as you do it well. The "Advertising and Marketing" chapter in *Start-Up Basics* covers advertising and marketing in detail, so we will skip over the dos and don'ts common to all advertising. In this section, we'll cover the important points you need to get across in ads for your staffing service. We'll also discuss the different types of advertising that work well for finding clients in this industry.

The Point Is...

To produce an effective ad, you must first make clients aware of the advantages of using a staffing service. These advantages include the following:

- *Pre-tested, pre-screened employees.* Clients get employees who are ready to work.
- *Reduced turnover.* Replacing permanent employees is expensive. All companies want to reduce turnover and its associated costs.
- *Savings of time and money.* There is no need for clients to invest in recruitment or human resources efforts.
- *"Tried and true" employees.* Clients get to try out prospective employees to see if they provide a good fit for the company.

Notice that the above points, while important, are very general in nature. In theory, they are true of any staffing company. Put them in your ad, by all means. Just don't imagine that they do anything to differentiate your service from other staffing services. The way you do that is by listing those features that set your company apart from the rest. Emphasize the benefits your clients receive from using your staffing service. Be sure to mention any of the following features if you offer them:

- *Bonded employees.* This can be a selling point, especially if theft or damage is a substantial risk for clients. (See Chapter 3 for details on bonding.)
- *Call-back guarantee.* Many services guarantee that they will call clients back within a specified time (such as 15 minutes).

> ### Bright Idea
> Stuck for ways to attract clients? Consider giving an "introductory offer" discount to companies you would like to have as customers. Handled appropriately, this strategy may work because people are often more willing to use a service if they can do it economically.

- *Customized services.* If you tailor any of the services you offer (screening, training techniques, etc.) to clients' needs, make sure to mention this fact.

- *Post-training assessment.* Many services test employees again after they've enhanced their skills. This way, clients get measurable results.

- *Unconditional guarantee.* Some services offer a money-back guarantee. This is another feature that attracts attention in an ad.

- *Well-trained employees.* If you offer employee training, make sure clients know this.

Make a list of these and any other features your service has to offer. Then, before you decide what the ad should look like, consider where you will place it.

Way to Go

We will now discuss some typical advertising strategies and how well they work for staffing services. Note that before you place any ad, you should know who will be reading your ad and what their major concerns are likely to be. This information will help you target your ad correctly.

- *Brochure.* A well-designed, high-quality brochure can be an effective advertising vehicle for your staffing company. Note, however, that brochures are generally expensive to produce and not always immediately necessary. Seattle entrepreneur Dyana Veigele didn't create a brochure for her firm until its fourth year, and now churns out a new one each year.

- *Direct mail.* This strategy works well in the industry. Choose your mailing list well, focusing on those companies whose size and industry sector make them likely prospects.

- *Internet.* Electronic ads on various industry-specific bulletin boards can be an effective way to advertise for the professional and technical sectors.

- *Newspaper.* This is a good method for some sectors of the staffing industry, but major newspapers may not be helpful in the professional or technical sectors.

- *Radio.* Most staffing services have not found radio to be an effective means of advertising.

- *Specialty publications.* Ads in these can help you target particular types of companies. Several of the owners we talked to advertise this way.

- *Telephone.* Some staffing services call existing clients to let them know about applicants currently available. Handled well, this can be an effective way to generate more business.

- *Television.* Consider cable television, which is less expensive and easier to localize than national television. Recruiting experts in the staffing industry consider cable television an effective option.

- *Trade journals.* These are most effective for attracting clients in the professional and technical industry sectors. For example, a legal staffing service can advertise in legal journals.

  The sample trade journal advertisement below is one that might appear in a business publication. This staffing service is marketing its computer programmers and other technicians to large companies.

- *Word-of-mouth.* This is the best kind of advertising. It's the most credible and definitely the least expensive! Dyana Veigele of Law Dawgs says her company kept a low advertising profile in the beginning. If you enter a market that has high competition like Seattle, you don't want to just bust down doors and say "Here we are." Many firms, she explains, have long-standing, loyal staffing relationships. Initially, her company relied heavily on word-of-mouth advertising.

- *Yellow Pages.* Most owners said their Yellow Pages ad is effective for recruiting employees, but not for attracting clients. In fact, some owners are suspicious of clients who find them via the Yellow Pages. These are often high-risk clients with bad credit.

Sample Trade Journal Advertisement

New Millennium Staffing Inc.

oo Century Blvd. • Normal, IL 61761

Speedy, reliable solutions to your toughest problems

- Temporary and Temp-to-Perm
- Tested and Trained Staff
- Bonding
- 30-Minute Call-Back Guarantee
- Customized Services

- Post-Training Assessment
- Expertise in All Computer Languages
- Programmers, Interface Designers, and More

Satisfaction guaranteed!
CALL (800) 000-5555

Win Friends and Influence People

Who you know, and who knows you, counts for a lot. All owners we talked to emphasized the importance of networking. You and your sales staff should do as much of it as possible. Networking is the major strategy that a sales staff uses for acquiring clients.

Following are some ways to expand your circle of business acquaintances:

- *Attend professional conferences.* Meeting professionals in your own, or a related, industry is always helpful.
- *Get involved in local charity work.* Besides being the right thing to do, helping with a local charity event can go a long way toward solidifying your community contacts.
- *Join professional organizations.* Local business organizations provide good networking opportunities. You can also join area business associations, including the chamber of commerce. All these ties can bring your firm increased visibility. (See the Appendix for a listing of some associations.)
- *Make frequent phone contact.* "The bottom line of the entire sales effort is you have to work hard at it," says Rita Zoller, who owns First Call Temporary Services. "You have to be on the phone; you have to be out there."

The Image of Success

How the public views your staffing service is important. A positive company image is especially crucial as staffing companies become more specialized.

To be successful, you need to work hard on your company's image. For one, you should invest heavily in computer technology. Your offices should also have "finishing touches" such as a fully furnished office, a receptionist, and a personalized promotional message for callers on hold. Finally, consider investing in the services of a marketing company to help develop an image for your business. The investment can pay for itself tenfold when everything your company sends out is coordinated and displays the company logo.

Bright Idea

Consider establishing relationships with other staffing companies. You can send any positions you can't fill to them, and vice versa. That's what Patricia Troy-Brooks' Advanced Staffing has done. "We want our customers to be satisfied and we want them to know, even if we're not going to make a dime on it, that they are most important to us," Troy-Brooks says.

Dyana Veigele's strategy for building her company's image began with its location. Her choice of a top bank building in downtown Seattle made it clear to both clients and applicants that her staffing service was a professional, upscale business. She relied on the quality of the employees she placed to help her earn a good reputation and to solidify her company's image.

The strategies mentioned above are all good ones. However, the best way to ensure a good image is to make certain that you deliver excellent customer service. This is the topic of the next section.

> ## Beware!
> Make sure all your office documents, whether they are brochures, applications, or simple business letters, are well-written and grammatically correct. Nothing creates a worse impression than sloppy documents. Take the time to proofread.

Customer Service—The Nature of the Best

The importance of excellent customer service can't be overemphasized. Repeat customers are the mainstay of any successful business, and this fact is especially true in the staffing services industry.

What are the distinguishing features of excellent customer service? Above all, staffing services bend over backward to do what clients want. What's more, small accounts can grow your business, so pay as much attention to them as you do to large accounts. And always look for new opportunities to be of service. Those who build relationships have better long-term prospects. Client-centered policies will help your company retain a loyal customer base.

- *Anticipate clients' needs.* Because nearly 70 percent of the industry consists of light industrial and administrative work, differentiation between staffing companies is not always easy to achieve. The successful companies are those that provide proactive customer service. People who have been successful in this business have done so because they've been out ahead of what their customers need. You should help clients predict what their future staffing needs will be.

  Anticipating what clients will need means knowing the industry—and knowing it well. For tips on educating yourself, see "Information, Please..." on the next page.

> ## Smart Tip
> Remember that every choice you make—from the employees you send out on the job to your company logo to the business paper you choose (which should be high-quality paper in a neutral shade)—reflects your taste and company image.

- *Be honest.* It's crucial to be forthright with customers about employees. If you don't have the right person, tell clients to call their backup service. Honesty also means admitting mistakes you've made and not pretending to know information you don't know.

  Note, however, that you have a right to expect honesty in return. Providing good customer service

Bright Idea

If you're striking out in one industry specialty, or simply want to expand your business, look for a new but related field to enter. In Indianapolis, Rita Zoller's First Call Temporary Services, geared toward industrial companies, is now serving the auto industry as well.

Information, Please...

One of the best ways to keep customers coming back to your staffing service is to be constantly on the lookout for new ideas and ways to improve the services you provide. We have mentioned more than once the importance of staying informed about the staffing industry. So what are the best ways to do that? All of the following will help you keep up, not only with a quickly changing industry, but also with factors that affect it, like the economy.

- ○ *Join professional organizations.* The American Staffing Association (ASA) is the major industry association. See the Appendix for a list of other associations.
- ○ *Go to professional conferences.* The ASA and other organizations have annual conferences that are valuable sources of information.
- ○ *Invest in an hour (or more) with an industry consultant.* Someone who knows the industry, but who is outside your company, can often be helpful.
- ○ *Read everything you can.* Owners we spoke to read a variety of publications related to the staffing industry, as well as to the economy in general (see the Appendix for a list of publications).
- ○ *Subscribe to at least one professional newsletter or journal.* As we have already said, reading is important.
- ○ *Take a course in some aspect of the staffing industry.* For example, the ASA offers a class on employment law. Several owners we interviewed took that course and said it was extremely helpful.

Making sure you and your employees are well informed will help keep excitement and energy levels high, which is what you need to maintain peak performance at your staffing service.

does not mean tolerating unacceptable business practices from clients. If a client habitually misrepresents the demands of a job in order to lower the billing rate, consider dropping that client. Renegotiating a billing rate, reassigning the position, and other trouble-shooting strategies all consume time and energy.

- *Do what you say you're going to do.* Chances are, your service will make certain promises and commitments to clients. Make sure you keep these commitments to the letter.

- *Find out what clients want.* To do this, you have to ask questions. Rather than presenting clients with a service program you've decided is good, ask them what they consider good service to be. "Let clients tell you what they want," says Rita Zoller. "They will tell you if you ask them."

- *Give clients what they want.* Once you find out what clients want, give it to them. It's as simple as that (and as complicated). Sometimes, however, your service will be unable to do this. If you don't have anyone who can do the job well, either tell the client to call a different staffing company or—better yet—call one yourself. This strategy will boost client confidence and will enhance your business reputation.

- *Keep in contact with the client.* All owners mentioned the importance of staying in touch. Train your staff to be proactive about making calls to clients to find out how employees are doing.

- *Modify your customer service.* An ability to change policies that aren't working well is important. "That's an advantage of a small company," says Rita Zoller. "You can change on a dime." Learn to gauge how much attention a client wants and needs from you. "Too much service is as bad as too little," she warns. After all, people are busy, including your clients. Don't be like the waitperson who comes to inquire every five minutes.

- *Satisfy the customer.* All owners mentioned this point. If you do everything else we've just mentioned, you should end up with happy customers.

Follow the advice in this chapter and use your start-up period to expand your knowledge, solidify your industry and community contacts, and develop a reputation you can be proud of. If you do this, profits will come your way. To make sure you hang onto your profits, check out the financial management suggestions in Chapter 9.

Beware!

Some companies bump up job descriptions on the theory that if they request more skills than they actually need, they'll get higher-quality employees. Even though clients may pay more, you don't want bored employees or wasted talents. Make sure you give accurate reports of employee abilities and that you get accurate job requirements.

9

The Ins and Outs of Financial Management

In this chapter, we will focus on the financial rewards and frustrations of the staffing industry. You'll learn about revenues, markups, and profit margins. And we'll show you how to price your services and how to stay profitable. The "Financial Statements" and "Financial Management" chapters in *Start-Up Basics* provide in-depth information on markup and gross profit margin—and financial management in general.

▲

Sum Total

How much can you expect your business to make in gross sales? These figures vary wildly in the staffing services industry. Staffing experts say that privately held companies probably average somewhere around $750,000 per year. But we talked to several owners whose businesses make close to $15 million in gross sales. More than one owner topped $1 million in sales the very first year.

Marking It Up

The profit for staffing services is in the markup they add to the price of an employee's labor. There is a huge range for markups in the staffing industry. In fact, several owners noted that although industry markups have slipped in recent years, markups can remain high even in a slumping economy because there aren't that many qualified applicants to work with. In addition, today's workplace requires more skills and therefore more training. Wide markup ranges exist even within the same company. For example, the markup for PDQ Personnel Services in Los Angeles is anywhere from 25 to 75 percent.

To determine the amount of markup you can earn for a particular type of placement, you'll need to consider all the following factors:

- *Amount of competition.* If you have relatively little competition in the type of staffing you do or the training you provide, you can get a generous markup. On the other hand, if you have a lot of competition, your markup is more likely to be average for your industry sector and your area. For example, Seattle's Law Dawgs has a markup that runs between 55 and 70 percent. Owner Dyana Veigele knows of a legal staffing service in nearby Portland, Oregon, that gets a 75 percent markup. "That would be great," she says, "but realistically in Seattle we can't go that high because there's just too much competition."

- *Client relationship.* A client who gives you a lot of business should get a more favorable billing rate, which means your markup will be lower. For example, Veigele's company has gone as low as a 20 percent markup. "Sometimes we just want to make the placement for that client, and the markup's not going to be great," she says. Law Dawgs does give special rates to high-volume clients or to clients that have been with the company for a long time.

- *Industry sector.* In general, niche markets (e.g., IT) produce higher markups than do traditional staffing markets

> **Stat Fact**
> Some 90 percent of staffing companies provide free training to their temporary employees, according to the ASA. And 70 percent of temporary employees say they gain new skills through their assignments.

(e.g., clerical). Veigele notes that occasionally her firm's markup can approach 75 percent for a computer company client.

- *Local standards.* Your service's geographical location will also dictate, in part, what kind of markup you can get. For example, although markups in the industrial sector range from 26 percent to 50 percent in the Indianapolis area, Rita Zoller notes that markups in the same sector appear to be a little higher in Chicago.

Belonging to industry organizations and engaging in other forms of networking can help you discover what kinds of markups similar staffing services are getting in your area. The more information you can collect about this, the better.

Comfortable Margins

Profit margins are healthy in the staffing services industry. Net profit margins (profit margins after you pay operating costs) in general staffing services can run from 4 to 10 percent. And what if your company doesn't do general staffing, but instead operates in one of the niche markets? "The sky's the limit," says Zoller. Nevertheless, staffing industry profit margins vary widely. According to the ASA, a profit margin of even 5 percent, especially in the first few years of operation, is respectable.

Dyana Veigele says her company's profit margin hasn't been affected too terribly during the lean years because she's gotten smarter about streamlining. She notes that the business still has the potential to be highly profitable.

One owner estimates that her gross profit margins runs about 46 percent. After operating costs, her net profit margin is probably 25 to 27 percent before taxes. She adds that without the permanent placement income, her profit margins would run 9 to 11 percent. Temporary employees are her mainstay, and they are also how she gets a lot of her permanent placements. But the latter really beef up the bottom line, she says.

The Price Is Right

How should you figure out how much to charge your clients? In this section, we'll discuss charges for three types of placements that happen routinely in the staffing services industry. These include temporary, temp-to-perm, and permanent placement.

1. *Temporary placement.* For this kind of billing, use the following three steps:
   a. Figure out the pay rate (how much you will need to pay an employee).
   b. Apply the markup that you think you can reasonably get (see "Marking It Up" on page 104).
   c. The total is the billing rate.

   For example, if you are paying a talented interface designer $50 per hour and decide you can get a markup of 80 percent, here is the math:

80 percent of $50 = .80 \times 50 = 40$
(This means your markup will be $40 per hour.)
$40 + $50 = 90 (This is your hourly billing rate.)

2. *Temp-to-perm placement.* Some staffing services do not charge at all for this kind of placement, especially if they have had several months in which to make a profit from a temporary employee's labor before the client hires that employee permanently. For example, Rita Zoller has not traditionally charged clients for temp-to-perm hiring. She estimates that in the industrial sector, only about 5 percent of her competitors charge a fee at hiring. "But we are going to be changing this," she explains, citing the labor shortage and the increased difficulty in recruiting as the reasons for the change.

But some staffing services do charge a fee for temp-to-perm placements. This is reasonable because when a client hires one of your employees, you then cease to make any profit from that worker, in whom you may have invested a considerable amount of time and money to recruit and train.

If you charge a temp-to-perm fee, how much should that be? Like so much else in this industry, it depends. In general, the harder it is to recruit and train employees for the type of placement you do, the higher your fees will be. The same four factors that help determine your markup rate (i.e., amount of competition, client relationship, industry sector, and local standards) will also affect your temp-to-perm fees. As an example, legal staffing services usually charge 10 to 15 percent of the gross annual salary that the worker will be making.

3. *Permanent placement.* If you place employees permanently right off the bat, without employing them as temporary workers first, then the fee you charge the client company will be much higher than it is for temp-to-perm placement. This, too, is logical, because you'll have no other opportunity to make a profit on the labor of a person you've recruited, tested, and possibly trained.

Not all the owners we interviewed do permanent placement. Those who do charge higher percentages for higher gross salaries or wages. For example, one staffing service owner charges a permanent placement fee of 1 percent per $1,000 of payroll. So for an employee who will make $20,000 per year, the

Beware!
Most clients understand that the more skills they request, the higher the bill rate. So sometimes companies request fewer skills than they actually need. They might call for a receptionist with light typing when they really need an executive secretary with heavy duty word processing. If this is the case, renegotiate the billing rate. If a company does this too often, consider dropping that company as a client.

company charges the client 20 percent of $20,000, which amounts to $4,000. Law Dawgs generally charges 10 to 20 percent of the expected gross annual salary or wages. Why, you may ask, are fee rates for higher-salaried employees at the top of the percent range? Because it's harder to find those employees, and the recruitment costs are much higher.

Make sure that whatever type of placement you do provides you with enough profit to cover the costs associated with those employees. This is one way to ensure that your business remains profitable. We'll now go on to examine a few more ways to stay in the black.

> **Tip...**
>
> ### Smart Tip
> When you hire new temporary employees, be sure they understand the importance of letting you know if one of your clients offers them a permanent job. Also, you should have an agreement in writing with clients that they will not hire away workers without paying you a temp-to-perm fee (sometimes called a conversion fee).

Avoiding Red Ink

There are several effective means of ensuring that your company stays out of the red. Following are some of them.

- *Control your accounts receivable.* Make sure you do not allow clients to owe you money for long periods of time. What's the secret to this? Negotiate the shortest possible payment schedule, put it into the client contract, and then stay in contact with that client.

  "Typically, you might see receivables in the 45- to 50-day range, according to the ASA. So, if you are going to pay your employees every week, and it takes you (for example) 47 days to collect, you have 40 days' worth of "float time" that you have to cover. Nevertheless, as you gain industry experience, try to negotiate a quick turnaround right from the beginning. If you can trade your invoices for a check, your company won't have to wait for clients to pay bills. A new company might also find it worthwhile to accept a lower billing rate in return for immediate payment.

  Aim to have close to 100 percent of your money within 30 days for better cash flow. The waiting period can be even shorter if client contracts stipulate a 10-day paying period. Controlling accounts receivable can help make or break your company, and it, in turn, can depend on the customer service your company provides. So make sure you stay in touch with clients.

- *Diversify your clients.* Avoid allowing your staffing service to become too dependent on just a few large clients. If those clients take their business elsewhere, you could end up in big trouble. One owner's strategy for financial stability is to constantly monitor her business mix.

▲

- *Diversify your niches.* Operating within more than one niche is a good way to diversify your clients. This strategy is also a good hedge against economic downturns. Several owners we spoke to branched out into technical niches, to take advantage of Y2K work (which earned good money for employees and staffing companies alike) and gain a safeguard against a downturn in a different industry sector.

- *Plan for rapid growth.* You should assume that at some point you may need a quick infusion of cash. Why is this? If you are a rapidly growing company, that means your payables are going up rapidly (because you've got more workers). Even though your sales are also increasing, the delay (until clients pay you) means you're racing to catch up. This is a "good" problem, but you will probably need a line of credit to deal with it. How much credit? If you do about, say, $750,000 worth of business in a year and it takes you 60 days (or one-sixth of a year) to collect money from your clients, use the following equation:

$$\$750{,}000 \times 1/6 = \$750{,}000 \div 6 = \$125{,}000$$

This means that, at any given time, you have $125,000 that you are trying

---

Temporary Treasure

Keep in mind that, depending on the industry sector you work in, your profit margin on a good employee will decrease over time (or end altogether). For example, Rita Zoller, who does about 78 percent of her business in the industrial sector, typically employs workers for several months. After that, the client company hires them, thus avoiding the need for raises during temp employment. When clients subsequently hire employees permanently, they often give raises as part of the hiring process.

Even if you don't lose good employees to permanent jobs, your profit margins on them generally decrease. After all, even though many employee raises can be "passed on" to the client, you can't always charge a client more just because you've decided to give a valued employee a raise. The extra money you pay that employee may come out of your profit margin. Giving an employee a raise means you are willing to make less money on that employee than you make on others.

This is a valid strategy for keeping good employees. But remember that you must allow for raises within the markup amount that you choose. Too low a markup, such that you can't afford to give an employee a raise, means you will eventually lose that employee, who will justifiably go to another service to get the desired raise.

to collect from clients. Under these circumstances, you would need a line of credit that is at least $125,000.

If you are not able to get a line of credit from a bank, as many new companies are not, you can get a funding company to help you meet your payroll, or you can sell your invoices to a factoring company (see Chapter 4 for more information on these options). But whatever you do, investigate your options well before you are in sudden, dire need of additional capital.

Beware!
Several interviewees mentioned that doctors' offices and law firms are notoriously slow at paying bills. One said the only doctors and lawyers she accepts as clients are those who have business managers.

- *Price your services accurately.* As we mentioned in the previous section, make sure you have given yourself enough of a markup to cover all operating costs (including your own salary) and still leave a small cushion for unexpected expenses.

- *React promptly to changes.* Although you should do what you can to anticipate change, sometimes this is impossible and the only thing left to do is react. Just make sure you don't wait too long. For example, in Indianapolis, First Call Temporary Services does volume business with large company clients. In a couple of cases, owner Rita Zoller opened offices to service specific clients. In each case, business from those clients later disappeared. The first time that happened, she did not close the office quickly enough. "We learned from that," she says. The next time it happened, Zoller reacted more quickly.

The lesson? Although you should guard against "knee jerk" reactions, remember that a reluctance to act can also create problems for your business. And one distinct advantage of a small company is that it can often react more quickly to change than a larger company can, putting you squarely back on your feet.

Beware!
A significant Catch-22 in this industry, more than in most, is that growing too fast presents a very real hazard. "You think you're getting ahead, because you're making more placements," says Dyana Veigele of Law Dawgs, "but it takes you a while to catch up with your billing. If you suddenly get a huge request, you could be dead in the water. Because the thing is, you have got to pay your people, even if you're not paid by your clients."

- *Review financing options.* Often, more established businesses can renegotiate loan terms or find new sources of loans. Look into your options. For example, in the early years of your business, you might aim to pay off high-interest loans and replace expensive early financing with a bank line of credit.

- *Expect slow periods.* The staffing services industry is, in some ways, a lot like retailing. Some months are busier than others. Also, natural forces like snow or earthquakes affect your employees—and your business. Both don't get paid if your employees can't get work. Make sure you have a cushion to fall back on when a slow period hits.

Now that you have a handle on your finances, it's time to take a look at other factors crucial to the success of your staffing company. This is a major topic of Chapter 10.

Whatever
It Takes
Finding Success

The first topics we'll cover in this chapter are how not to fail and how to do effective trouble-shooting. Then, as you may have guessed from the title of this chapter, we're going to focus on success. Finally, we'll peek at tea leaves to discuss the probable future of the staffing industry.

Thumbs Down

What are the major reasons people fail in the staffing services industry? Many of the problems we list below are common to all start-up businesses but are particularly true for staffing services. They include the following:

> **Smart Tip**
>
> Temporary employees often forget that the staffing service is their employer, not the client company. Showing your appreciation to your temporary staff (see Chapter 8) not only makes them feel good, but it also reminds them that you are their employer and should be informed if they are sick or if some other work-related problem arises.

- *Inadequate financing.* Several interviewees mentioned this one. It's a problem in any industry, but particularly in this one. Why? In this business, cash is king. You must have your financial house in order to weather periodic storms and without fail you must meet payroll.

- *Inadequate insurance.* This is an industry with a lot of potential liability problems. One expensive claim can wipe you out if you are underinsured. Re-evaluate your insurance needs periodically.

- *Inadequate planning.* This is another common problem, intensified in this industry because of its rapid growth rate. You need to plan for sudden growth.

- *Lack of temporary workers.* Because the skill and labor of your temporary workers is the major product you sell, this can be a serious problem. Make sure you are constantly recruiting.

- *Poor customer service.* You must satisfy your clients. It's that simple. Follow the strategies outlined in Chapter 8.

- *Underestimation of the time commitment required.* As is usually the case with a new business, you have to put in a lot of time getting it off the ground. "Be prepared to put in 80 hours per week starting out," says Dyana Veigele, who owns Law Dawgs in Seattle. "You eat it, you drink it, you sleep it; it's on your mind constantly." A staffing business demands long hours—something you have to accept from the get-go.

- *Unsatisfactory workers.* If the employees you place are unqualified or unprofessional, your staffing service will not have a good reputation. Make sure you have effective testing and evaluation procedures.

Nobody Knows the Trouble I've Seen

The staffing industry is not immune to Murphy's Law. "If it can go wrong, it has," says Rita Zoller, who owns First Call Temporary Services in Indianapolis. Expect that you'll need to trouble-shoot from time to time. Following are some of the problems you may encounter, along with suggestions for dealing with them.

- *Client dissatisfaction.* If a client indicates dissatisfaction with an employee, many staffing service owners do not charge that client. You may have to use your judgment on this, however, if the client waits longer than the customary four hours before notifying your service. Whatever you decide, you must pay the employee.

- *No-show employee.* You might give no-shows one strike before crossing them off your employee list—unless they have a good, documented reason for not showing up, such as a trip to the hospital or a family emergency. Under those circumstances, you might give them a second chance.

- *Employee cancellation.* This is annoying and time wasting for both the staffing service and the client. Send termination letters to employees who show a pattern of cancellations. But first, listen to the reason, and give them a few chances. Document the occurrence in the computer each time, and work quickly to find a replacement worker for the client. This is the critical point: Make replacing workers your top priority.

- *Missing time sheet.* Getting employees to turn in their time sheets on schedule can be an ongoing hassle. "When payroll is due, we are invariably on the phone calling people for their time sheets," says Veigele. "It puts us back in our billing." Another reason time sheets can be missing at payroll time is that they occasionally get lost.

  The simplest solution to a temporarily missing time sheet is to have firm deadlines for handing in time sheets. Employees who miss the deadline don't get paid that week. If you, like many owners, are unable to bring yourself to enforce this type of policy, then you can get the employee to phone in the information so that the payroll division can cut the check. Do not, however, hand over the check before you have the employee's signed time sheet in your hands.

  If a time sheet is lost, then someone in your office should fill out a "missing time sheet report" (virtually all industry software provides a form like this) using the employee's phoned-in information. Verify it with the client and then supply the payroll division with that form as a substitute for the time sheet.

- *Inaccurate job description.* Your personnel coordinator (or whatever that person's title is) gives out assignments based on the information the client company provides, and sometimes that information is inaccurate. Job duties that turn out to be different than the client previously stated can end up wasting an employee's time and your money. Law Dawgs attempts (usually successfully) to remedy that by filling out a profile of an assignment and faxing or

> **Smart Tip**
>
> *Tip...*
>
> Make sure you keep good records of everything, whether it relates to financing, insurance, planning, or time management. Sometimes, past records will allow you to make helpful predictions.

e-mailing it back to the client for verification. Employees are justified in calling your service and asking either for someone to replace them (if the job requirements are substantially less or more than the employee is capable of) or a higher pay rate (if the job requirements are more than stated but the employee has the necessary skills). In the latter case, you will have to renegotiate with the client company and establish a higher billing rate.

- *Client unreliability.* Clients can be unreliable in several different ways. They can give you problems at billing time by paying late. This could be either because they are simply bad at paying bills or because

Beware!

If an employee accuses a supervisor from a client company of sexual harassment, threats, misplaced blame for a project gone wrong, or anything else, you should do the following three things: (1) reassign the employee; (2) get some written communication from both employee and client; and (3) keep a record of the problem and what you did to correct it.

they are insolvent. But often your bills are paid even if a client is in financial trouble. That means when the client goes out of business, you are caught by surprise. Determining how financially solid your client companies are can be tough, if not downright impossible. Law Dawgs had one of its biggest clients, the fourth largest law firm in the area, suddenly go out of business. Clients can also be difficult for employees to work with, either because of the supervisory staff or because of policies or attitudes toward temporary workers.

What can you do to minimize these types of problems with clients? You can get references on firms you deal with, as does Law Dawgs. Dyana Veigele points out that, rather than being concerned only with making a placement, staffing services must provide the best possible working environment for the people they place. If her company is not comfortable with a client, they will turn down that client. Getting your temporary staff to evaluate the firms you send them to can also be helpful (see Chapter 6).

- *Employee steals from the client.* Theft is a serious problem, but this is where your bonding insurance will come in very handy. You do have that insurance, right? If you don't know what the heck we're talking about, go back to Chapter 3 and look at insurance coverage again. Bonding is crucial.

- *Employee steals your client list and your temporary employees list.* Aside from your personnel themselves, these two lists are probably the most valuable assets of your business. If an employee steals them, fill out a claim with your bonding company. If you can prove the theft, you should also take the employee to court.

- *Placement that ends sooner than expected.* A few hours is not a crucial difference, but if an employee's assignment ends much earlier than expected, that

It's the Law

Below are some pieces of legislation that all employers should be aware of. Make sure your staffing service is in compliance with all of the following:

○ *Americans with Disabilities Act of 1990.* This legislation prohibits discrimination based on a physical or mental handicap by employers engaging in interstate commerce.

○ *The Age Discrimination in Employment Act.* This act protects employees over age 40 from discrimination based on their age.

○ *The Equal Pay Act.* This document states that equal pay must be given to workers for equal work if the jobs they perform require the same skill and responsibility.

○ *Title VII of the Civil Rights Act of 1964.* This provision prohibits employment discrimination based on race, color, religion, sex, or national origin.

Keeping these laws in mind can help you avoid situations that might result in legal problems.

employee should be put at the top of the list for another assignment. Your ability to keep employees working for the promised length of time will do much to create a good reputation for your service. After all, your employees depend on the income you tell them they'll make from an assignment.

- *Placement that lasts longer than expected.* Under this circumstance, an employee is justified in asking you to find someone else to complete the assignment. After all, employees have schedules and other commitments, just as you do. However, if at all possible, the employee should give you a few days' notice to find a qualified replacement.

- *Employee hates the job.* This will happen occasionally. When you receive a "Please get me out of here" call, ask the employee to stay at the assignment until you can find a replacement. Then do so as quickly as possible.

An Ounce of Prevention

The best kind of trouble-shooting involves anticipating where problems may arise and dealing with them before they crop up. Make sure you have the following:

- *Good insurance coverage.* This should include, at the very least, liability insurance, errors and omissions insurance, and bonding insurance (see Chapter 3).

- *The right legal clauses.* You should have noncompete clauses in the contracts your permanent employees sign. You should also have a no-hire clause in client contracts. (See Chapter 2 for more information on these two clauses.) Finally, many bad situations can be avoided if your employees are aware of the things they should not agree to do. The backs of time sheets should contain the following three guidelines:

1. Employees may not be entrusted with cash or other valuables.

2. Employees may not be left alone on the premises.

3. Employees may not operate machinery or motor vehicles without the written consent of the service.

> **Smart Tip**
>
> *Tip...*
>
> Rita Zoller of First Call Temporary Services says the most important advice she can give to anyone starting up is to make sure you have good insurance, particularly workers' compensation and unemployment, and to control your accounts receivable. "Set up those receivables with a short-term turnaround," she advises.

The orientation material you pass out to employees should instruct them to say no if they are asked to do anything your service prohibits (see above). They should also refuse to do anything that jeopardizes their own health or financial well-being, such as the following:

- *Buy their own supplies.* Unless there is a special agreement in the contract, client companies are expected to furnish supplies.

- *Do anything illegal, like forging a signature.* Employees should inform your staffing service if a client asks them to perform an illegal task.

- *Operate in a hazardous work environment without the proper safety gear.* Your clients must be in compliance with the Occupational Safety and Health Act (OSHA), a federal law that requires employers to provide a workplace that is free of hazardous conditions.

- *Sign any document as a witness.* This could get an employee into legal trouble.

- *Work in a different capacity than stated in the contract.* If a job turns out to be different than previously agreed, the contract must be renegotiated.

- *Work on their own time.* Employees should not be expected to stay longer than the time they are being paid for.

- *Work without breaks.* Most states have a legal requirement that employees be given a 10- to 15-minute break every two hours.

Thumbs Up

Avoiding mistakes and fixing problems are important parts of building a successful company. But there are many more positive things you can do to strengthen your business. According to what our interviewees told us, the following tips are all keys to success in the staffing services industry:

- *Deliver superior customer service.* Remember to make your commitment to excellent customer service clear to all your employees, including your temporary ones. Rita Zoller says that in her experience, the crucial factors to success are how fast you fix problems and how good your service is.

- *Manage your finances effectively.* Take another look at our Chapter 9 suggestions for staying profitable. Cash flow is without question the paramount key to success.

> **⚠ Beware!**
> Clients who always pay late can wreak havoc on your company's financial stability. Be courteous and reasonable, but do not allow even important clients to systematically miss payment deadlines. This sets a bad precedent.

- *Be persistent.* Don't give up, even if business is slow at first. Plug away, and keep the rewards of business ownership in mind.

- *Be resilient.* Both Patty DeDominic, who owns PDQ Personnel Services in Los Angeles, and Dyana Veigele mentioned this one. "We're all going to take knocks," says DeDominic. "The successful people are those who keep getting up."

  Veigele advises new owners to learn to deal with ups and downs. "Some days you just feel like everything's gone wrong. People aren't working out on assignments; you're not getting any calls. And then other days you just feel on top of the world, that you're making your clients happy, and you're finding people work." Remember, she emphasizes, that each day is different. After all, this is part of the industry's appeal.

- *Hire good staff.* Make sure your permanent staff members' philosophies are similar to yours and to each others'. One secret to success is having a staff that is compatible, has a strong work ethic, and shows a strong customer orientation.

- *Educate yourself.* Keep up with business trends and legal practices. For example, consider getting training in legal issues of employment. The American Staffing Association offers an employment law seminar that earned praise from several staffing service entrepreneurs.

Quality Check

What does it take to be the owner of a successful staffing service? Our research shows that you need to have all, or most, of the following qualities:

- *Confidence.* When you deal with people as much as you will in this industry, you need enough confidence to not take the occasional conflict too personally.

- *Consistency.* This quality matters in a couple of ways. First, your service needs to perform well all the time, not just some of the time. In other words, you must provide consistently good placements. Also, your actions must be consistent with your words; do what you say you're going to do.

- *Discipline.* Many aspects of running a business require discipline. According to industry expert Mike Ban, a tightly disciplined sales approach is especially important.
- *Flexibility.* In this industry, every day is different than the last. You have to "go with the flow."
- *People skills.* Several owners and experts mentioned that this industry is all about relationships. "You have to like working with people or hang it up," says Veigele.
- *Persistence.* We covered this one in the previous section, but the idea bears repeating: Those who give up too easily will not succeed.
- *Sensitivity.* Genuine concern for both clients and employees is tough to fake successfully. If you have sensitivity, others will feel it and appreciate it.

Now that you know some of the qualities you need to maximize your chances for success, let's take a quick look at the probable future of the staffing industry.

Crystal Ball

What's ahead for the staffing industry? According to current trends and predictions, it looks as if the following are probable scenarios for the industry:

- *Renewed growth.* Current indicators show a slowly reviving economy, so the staffing industry should begin picking up steam again. According to the Bureau

---

You Can Say That Again

Imagine that a client calls your staffing service upset. An employee you placed can barely turn on the computer and is dressed inappropriately. "Here's the kiss of death," says Patricia Troy-Brooks, who owns Advanced Staffing in New Castle, Delaware. "The recruiter says, 'I'm surprised. We had her at IBM, and she did fine.'"

What is wrong with this response?

The message your recruiter just gave the client is that your staffing service questions the client's credibility. In effect, points out Troy-Brooks, your service is calling the client a liar.

What should you say instead?

Troy-Brooks advises you to apologize, stressing that your policy is to deliver the best possible service, and that you intend to make this up to the client. You should then replace the worker. "You have to satisfy the customer," she stresses. "You only get one shot to establish your credibility."

---

of Labor Statistics, the technical and professional (especially health) sectors of the industry should see the largest growth. The office and clerical sector should remain stable, with increased demand for computer skills. The industrial sector may experience a slight downturn as the number of manufacturing jobs continues to decline.

- *Decreased training costs.* The standardization of software products is an advantage for the staffing industry. According to the ASA, training costs in the industry may decline as staffing services will no longer need to provide extensive crosstraining. This means that training efforts can concentrate on finer and more advanced software processes.

Summing It Up

Finding the right niche, developing a strong client base, providing good customer service, and coping with a changing economy are all proven strategies for building a successful business. Periodically, you should ask yourself the following questions:

- Have I carefully analyzed the demand for my services, monitored the marketplace, and adjusted to changing conditions?
- Have I found a niche that provides me with enough diversity, yet also allows me to do what I do best?
- Do I have a sufficient cash reserve?
- Do I have a business plan that includes ideas for handling rapid growth?
- Are my placement services priced accurately?
- Have I kept my overhead costs to a minimum without sacrificing a professional image?
- Do I have employees, both permanent and temporary, who perform well?
- Does my company provide the kind of customer service that keeps clients coming back?

If you answered "yes" to all these questions, congratulations! Your staffing service has an excellent chance of succeeding. Any "no" answers indicate areas that need work. The good news is that identifying those areas makes it a lot easier to correct the problems and create a thriving business.

As the owners and experts we interviewed pointed out time and again, the staffing services industry offers exciting opportunities, rewarding work, and the certainty that you will never be bored.

Appendix
Staffing Service Resources

The Duchess of Windsor famously said that you can never be too rich or too thin. While that could be argued, it's true that you can never have too many resources. Therefore, for your consideration, here is a wealth of sources to investigate as you develop your plans for establishing a staffing service.

These sources are only the beginning. They are by no means the only sources available to you, nor can any claim total authority. Human resources is a volatile field, and businesses tend to move, change, fold, and expand. It's up to you to do your homework. Get out and start asking questions.

An extra word of advice: We strongly suggest you surf the Net for information. So long as you confirm your sources, you'll find abundant information about staffing and business trends on the Net, as well as related associations, books, conferences, and software.

Associations and Organizations

American Staffing Association (formerly NATSS), 277 S. Washington St., Alexandria, VA 22314, (703) 253-2020, www.staffingtoday.net, e-mail: asa@staffingtoday.net

Medor Staffing Services, 722A Fairmont Pkwy., Pasadena, TX 77504, (713) 941-0616, (800) 332-3310

Staffing Industry Analysts Inc. (publications, conferences, directories, research, and other resources), 881 Freemont Ave., Los Altos, CA 94024, www.staffingindustry.com.

U.S. Dept of Justice, Civil Rights Division, Office of Special Counsel Employer Information Hotline, (800) 255-8155, TDD: (800) 362-2735

World Wide Facilities Inc., 990 Stewart Ave., Garden City, NY 11530, (800) 245-9653, www.worldwidefacilities.com

Books

Co-Employment: Employer Liability Issues in Third Party Staffing Services Arrangements, Edward A. Lenz, American Staffing Association, 277 S. Washington St., Alexandria, VA 22314, (703) 253-2020, www.staffingtoday.net, e-mail: asa@staffingtoday.net

The Complete Guide to Contract Lawyering: What Every Lawyer and Law Firm Needs to Know About Temporary Legal Services, Deborah Arron and Deborah Guyol, Niche Press, www.decisionbooks.com

Manager's Guide to Employment Law, American Staffing Association, 277 S. Washington St., Alexandria, VA 22314, (703) 253-2020, www.staffingtoday.net, e-mail: asa@staffing today.net

Model Contracts, American Staffing Association, 277 S. Washington St., Alexandria, VA 22314, (703) 253-2020, www.staffingtoday.net, e-mail: asa@staffingtoday.net

Sex, Laws and Stereotypes, N. Elizabeth Fried, National Press Publications, 6901 W. 63rd St., 3rd Fl., Shawnee Mission, KS 66201, (800) 258-7246, www.natsem.com

Temping: The Insider's Guide, Richard M. Rogers, Simon & Schuster

The Temp Survival Guide: How to Prosper as an Economic Nomad of the Nineties, Brian Hassett, Carol Publishing Group

The Temp Track: Make One of the Hottest Job Trends for the 90s Work for You, Peggy O'Connell Justice, Peterson's Guides

VGM's Guide to Temporary Employment: A Practical Handbook for the Best Jobs, Lewis R. Baratz, VGM Career Books

Workforce 2000: Work and Workers for the 21st Century, William Johnston and Arnold Packer, Hudson Institute of Santa Barbara, (800) 582-4401, www.hudsoninstitute.org

Workforce 2020: Work and Workers in the 21st Century, Richard Judy and Carol D'Amico, Hudson Institute of Santa Barbara, (800) 582-4401, www.hudsoninstitute.org

Consultants

Cahill Consulting Group, P.O. Box 278, Cheshire, CT 06410, (203) 439-0267, www.accordingtodanny.com

World Wide Facilities Inc. (staffing industry insurance), 990 Stewart Ave., Garden City, NY 11530, (800) 245-9653, www.worldwidefacilities.com

Personality and Psychological Profiles

Drake P3—Predictive Performance Profiling System, Drake International, 400 Burrard St., 14th Fl., Vancouver, BC, V6C 3E2 CAN, (604) 643-1700, www.drakeintl.com

Empowerment Concepts Inc., 1276 N. Palm Canyon Dr., #205, Palm Springs, CA 92262, (760) 318-3710, www.rembrandtadvantage.com

Seminars and Videos

"Deconstructing Danny" (recruiting video), Cahill Consulting Group, P.O. Box 278, Cheshire, CT 06410, (203) 439-0267, www.accordingtodanny.com/products

"Staffing E-Trainer" (Web-based courses for staffing industry), Cumming, GA,(770) 740-0965, www.staffingetrainer.com,

Staffing Millennium Video Training Programs ("Temporary Help Sales," "Staffing Coordinator," "Staffing Manager," "Recruiting Manager"), Seminars By the Sea—International Staffing University, (877) 473-6731, www.semsea.com or www.istaffingu.com

"Workplace Harassment: How You Can Protect Against It," American Staffing Association, 277 S. Washington St., Alexandria, VA 22314, (703) 253-2020, fax: (703) 253-2053, www.staffingtoday.net, e-mail: asa@staffingtoday.net

Software

COATS, Sarach Technologies LLC, 4560 S. Blvd., #298, Virginia Beach, VA 23452, (800) 888-5894, www.coats95.com

Employment Services Command Center and *Time and Attendance Command Center (TACC)*, On-Site Off-Site Software, 1600 Sarno Rd., #16, Melbourne, FL 32935, (800) 765-0795, www.onsiteoffsite.com, e-mail: sales@onsiteoffsite.com

MyTTrax, Advanced Computer Technologies Inc., 3 Wentworth St., Nashua, NH 03060, (800) 57-TTRAX or (603) 595-1333, www.ttrax.com, e-mail: support@myttrax.com

MAESTRO Staffing Management System, eEmpACT Software, 1100 E. 80th St., Bloomington, MN 55420, (800) 456-5660, www.eempact.com (online demo available)

Pre-Valuate, Presenting Solutions Inc., 55 Santa Clara Ave., Oakland, CA 94610, (800) 547-7554, www.presol.com, e-mail: sales@prevaluate.com

Prove It! testing software, Kenexa, The Wold Building, 340 N. 12th St., #309, Philadelphia, PA 19107, (800) 935-6694 or (215) 546-7330, www.proveit.com, e-mail: proveit sales@kenexa.com

SkilMatch, SkilMatch Systems, (713) 627-1111, www.skilmatch.com, e-mail: info@skilmatch.com

Staffing Services, SkillCheck Inc., 113 Terrace Hall Ave., Burlington, MA 01803, (800) 648-3166, www.skillcheck.com, e-mail: sales@skillcheck.com

StaffTrax, Temp Trax, TraxStar Technologies LLC, 201 N. Civic Dr., #260, Walnut Creek, CA 94596, (800) 943-7759, www.traxstar.com

TempServ, Greenfield Software, 536 S. Lexington Ave., Burlington, NC 27215, (800) 226-9366, www.greenfieldsoftware.com, e-mail: gene@gfsw.com

TempWorks, TempWorks Software Inc., 3140 Neil Armstrong Blvd., #205, Eagen, MN 55121, (877) 452-0326, www.tempworks.com

Qwiz, 1805 Old Alabama Rd., #150, Roswell, GA 30076, (770) 650-8080, www.qwiz.com

Successful Staffing Services

Advanced Staffing, Patricia Troy-Brooks, 92 Read's Wy., #208, New Castle, DE 19720-1631, (302) 326-5400, www.advancedstaffing.net, e-mail: info@advancedstaffing.net

First Call Temporary Services, Rita Zoller, 6910 Hillsdale Ct., Indianapolis, IN 46250, (317) 596-3280

Law Dawgs Inc., Dyana Veigele, Washington Mutual Tower, 1201 Third Ave., 29th Fl., Seattle, WA 98101, (206) 224-8244, www.lawdawgs.com, e-mail: seattle@lawdawgs.com

PDQ Personnel Services Inc., Patty DeDominic, 5900 Wilshire Blvd., #400 and #450, Los Angeles, CA 90036, (323) 938-3933, www.pdqcareers.com, e-mail: info@pdqcareers.com

Staffing Team Inc., George Sotos, 2835 N. Sheffield, #238, Chicago, IL 60657, (773) 880-8849, www.staffingteam.com, e-mail: info@staffingteam.com

Trade Journals

American Staffing Association: Staffing Success (bimonthly magazine), Staffing Week (weekly newsletter), Staffing Law (updates three times a year), 277 S. Washington St., Alexandria, VA 22314, (703) 253-2020, www.staffingtoday.net, e-mail: asa@staffingtoday.net

Staffing Industry Analysts Inc. Newsletters: *Staffing Industry Report, IT Services Business Report, Staffing Industry Employment Bulletin, Staffing Industry Commercial News, Staffing Industry Healthcare News;* Magazines: *SI Review; Contingent Workforce Strategies Research/Data: Staffing Industry Sourcebook;* Directories: *Staffing Industry Supplier Directory, Staffing Industry Sourcebook,* 881 Fremont Ave., Los Altos, CA 94024, (800) 950-9496, www.staffingindustry.com

Web Sites

The following are popular job listing and resume posting databases:

America's Job Bank (job listings only), www.ajb.dni.us

Career City, www.careercity.com

Career Builder, www.careerbuilder.com

Monster Board, www.monsterboard.com

DICE (tech job listings only), www.dice.com

Glossary

Applicant: an individual seeking temporary employment with a staffing service

Assign: the act of sending a temporary employee to work on the premises of a client of the temporary staffing service

Assignment: the period of time during which a temporary employee is working on a customer's premises

Availability list: also known as a hot list, a list of temporary employees currently available for assignment

Billing rate: the rate at which the staffing service bills the client

Conversion fee: a fee paid by a company to a staffing service when hiring one of that service's employees on a permanent basis

Coordinator: a permanent employee of a staffing service who assigns temporary employees to work on the customer's premises

Employee leasing: an ongoing, permanent arrangement whereby a business transfers its employees to the payroll of a "leasing organization," after which the employees are leased back to their original employer to work in the same capacity as before. The leasing organization acts as an outsourced human resources department. Employee leasing is the principle occupation of a professional employer organization (PEO).

▲

Employment agency: a business whose purpose is to bring a job seeker and a prospective employer together for a permanent employment relationship

Fill rate: the proportion of work orders for which a staffing service is able to find temporary employees

Hot list: see *availability list*

Invoice: the bill sent to a client

Liquidated damages: the monies paid by staffing service clients under an agreement in which the client agrees not to hire the temporary employee within some specified period of time and to pay damages for breach of that promise in the agreed-upon amount

No-hire clause: a clause in which clients agree not to hire temporary employees prematurely, or to pay damages if they do

Noncompete clause: a clause in staffing services' permanent employees' contracts that states that those employees cannot either start their own staffing company or go to work for a competing staffing company within a certain period of time and within a certain specified geographical radius

Outsourcing: farming out to another company some function(s) a company would normally perform itself

Pay rate: the rate at which the staffing service pays an employee

Payroll: the salaries and wages paid to employees

Payrolling: a colloquial term describing a situation whereby the customer, rather than the temporary staffing service, recruits an individual and asks the temporary staffing service to employ the individual and assign him or her to the customer on a temporary basis

Permanent placement: the act of sending an employee to work for a client permanently, such that the worker is now the employee of the client rather than the staffing company

Shopping: a colloquial term for the practice of using devious means (e.g., posing as a client) to find out another staffing company's policies and procedures

Temp-to-perm: the practice of sending temporary employees on an assignment hoping to ultimately place them in a permanent position with the customer

Temporary employee: an employee who does not make a commitment to an employer to work on a regular, ongoing basis but instead is free to accept or reject assignments. A temporary employee is obligated only to complete a particular assignment once one is accepted, but has no obligation to accept further assignments.

Temporary staffing service: an organization engaged in the business of furnishing its own employees ("temporaries") to handle customers' temporary staffing needs and special projects

Time sheet: a sheet (signed by the client) that details the days and hours a temporary employee has worked

Work order: the order received from a customer for the services of a temporary staffing company

Index